WHAT A WAY TO SPEND A WAR

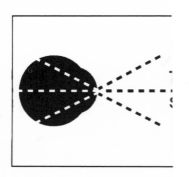

WHAT A WAY TO SPEND A WAR

NAVY NURSE POWS
IN THE PHILIPPINES

DOROTHY STILL DANNER

G.K. Hall & Co.
Thorndike, Maine

Published in 1997 by arrangement with Naval Institute Press.

G.K. Hall Large Print Paperback Collection.

The text of this Large Print edition is unabridged.
Other aspects of the book may vary from the original edition.

Set in 16 pt. Plantin by Warren S. Doersam.

Printed in the United States on permanent paper.

Library of Congress Cataloging in Publication Data

Danner, Dorothy Still, 1914–
    What a way to spend a war : Navy nurse POWs in the
    Philippines / Dorothy Still Danner.
        p.   cm.
    ISBN 0-7838-2021-6 (lg. print : sc)
    1. Danner, Dorothy Still, 1914–   .   2. World War, 1939–1945
— Prisoners and prisons, Japanese.   3. Prisoners of war —
Philippines — Biography.   4. Prisoners of war — United States —
Biography.   5. World War, 1939–1945 — Personal narratives,
American.   6. Nurses — United States — Biography.   I. Title.
[D805.P8D36   1995]
940.54'7252'092—dc21
    [B]   96-44456

Dedicated to those who were there,
Non intendo facere offensionum

CONTENTS

ACKNOWLEDGMENTS

I could not have written this book without my Navy nurse peers, other ex-POW Army and Navy personnel, and civilian internees who have shared their memories with me. The diaries and accounts of Drs. "Boyle," "Kleinfeldt," and "Mansfield" were a tremendous contribution.

Because our experiences under the Japanese thumb intermingled with the military prisoners so close by, I felt it was important that they be included in this story. Thus, except for notes that were slipped between some of us and our Navy men and what we heard, directly or indirectly, all information related to the Pasay Elementary School, Bilibid prison, and Cabanatuan is from the well-known journal kept by Medical Records Pharmacist's Mate 2c Robert Kentner. He continued to keep the daily log as ordered by the Japanese, secreting a more definitive account for himself. I have named him "Bornowski," for this book, parts of which have been fictionalized.

After a hiatus of half a century, literary license has been necessary. I cannot remember every detail, yet I hope my peers, nurses and civilians alike, will not have reason to wonder if they and I were in the same war. Personalities are amalgamated, and names have been changed except for the Japanese, some of those in the public domain, and my own.

PROLOGUE

It was Friday, 23 February. Just one more night, then back on the day shift. I took the five-day-old baby into the linen closet where it was a bit warmer. "You started off on the wrong foot, didn't you, little princess?" I cooed, hurriedly changing her diaper. "You're like a defeathered chicken on Mom's sink, ready for the stew pot." As her unfocusing eyes tried to locate the sound of my voice, I added, "No need to worry. You're too tiny to make much of a meal. Maybe if we fatten you up a bit?"

Overly diluted powdered milk was a poor substitute for mother's milk, but it would have to do, and I cuddled the blanket-wrapped baby closely as I cautiously tried to bottle-feed her. The infant nipple had long passed the stage when it should have been thrown out. Not only was it too soft, the opening was much too big for such a watery formula.

"Careful there, little lady," I whispered, putting her on my shoulder to burp her.

The night passed slowly, but at last dawn was breaking. While I sat at the desk in my regulation

11

Navy sweater, a ragged blanket over my knees, the orderlies were beginning to make preparations for early morning care.

"2/23/45," I wrote on each patient's chart, and made routine progress notes.

As the sky began to lighten, Jimmy went doggedly from bed to bed, emptying and refilling the water glasses, and another orderly came on duty. By 0650, the kitchen crew had a fire going in an effort to eke out nourishment from overworked bones. Nurses on the day's first shift were getting ready to take over.

"Will ya look at those lousy Japs?" Jimmy grumbled, as the garrison assembled in front of their quarters on Roosevelt Road.

"Yeah," I said. "We could do calisthenics, too, if we were as well fed as they are."

"Nurse, what do you suppose that is?" a patient asked.

"I can't imagine," I answered as we watched a column of pinkish smoke ascend into a windless sky. "It's colorful, to say the least."

"Sounds as though some of our planes are out there again."

"Sure does." With a yawn, I went over to check on the baby. Then suddenly —

Oh, dear God! They're going to kill us!

I grabbed the blanket-wrapped baby to protect her from the frightening sound of machine guns, and with the orderlies, I rushed over to peek out the front door at what sounded like war tanks about to break down the sawali-covered fence.

I held the little princess tighter still, with the deafening roar of nine C-47s circling the camp at low altitude. A bold banner attached to the fuselage of the lead plane read RESCUE!

1

BECOMING A NURSE

I think my mother would have liked to become a nurse herself, but nursing was the farthest thing from my mind when I was eighteen years old. I saw myself as a costume designer for the Warner Brothers Studios, but Mother had different ideas. Tuition was required for most nursing schools, and my parents couldn't afford that.

In any event, I tolerantly tagged along when she went to see the director of nurses at the Los Angeles General County Hospital. Much to her delight, I became a "probie" student nurse. As such, I had room and board and was paid $4.00 per month plus uniforms. As a regular student, I was paid $8.00 per month.

This stiff three-year course gave me a real sense of responsibility. From people of all ages I learned the true meaning of death and dying, and their gratitude for whatever I could do for them. There was so much to learn in medicine, and what better place could I have been than this hospital with its wide range of cases that included contagious diseases private nursing schools never saw.

Finally armed with a graduation pin and certified as a Registered Nurse, I was ready to face the outside world. I tried special duty nursing, worked in a doctor's office for a short while, and then worked in surgery at the Hollywood Hospital, but when the latest copy of the *American Journal of Nursing* crossed my path, I noticed application forms for both the Army and the Navy Nursing Corps. Certain that I was wasting a three-cent stamp, I sent one to the Navy. As far as I know, it had a total of about four hundred nurses on active duty, these from the entire nation. What I didn't know was that both the services were in the process of enlarging their nurse corps because of the critical situation in Europe. Needless to say, I jumped with joy when I received a letter from the Navy's Bureau of Medicine and Surgery:

YOU ARE HEREBY ORDERED TO APPEAR AT THE SAN DIEGO NAVY HOSPITAL FOR A PHYSICAL EXAMINATION ON 20 DECEMBER 1937 AT . . .

This I passed with flying colors, and as a result, I spent my first two-year tour of duty, 1938 and 1939, right in my own back yard. But having attained my RN hardly made me a worldly woman, a fact quickly recognized by the corpsmen and enlisted patients, and what fun they had with their seagoing jargon that went right over my head.

"Now hear this, you swabbies!" they would say just loud enough for me to hear. "Batten down the hatches on the double! Here comes a nor'-easter!"

They accused me of being a bosun's mate and of "running a helluva tight slip, er, ship," but regardless of the needling, I was thrilled to be a part of Uncle Sam's Navy with its traditional military rituals. It meant a new circle of nurse friends. We were professionally wiser, but still young, silly, and full of laughter. My three special friends were Adelma, Hazel, and Bonnie.

It was wonderful duty in itself, even without all the other exciting things to do. Who could possibly be bored with so many young doctors and a repository of aviation cadets on North Island? There were dinners, dances, and grunion hunting, not to mention golf, tennis, and trips to the Palomar Observatory. But oh, how quickly two years passed!

"Did you want to see me?" I asked when the chief nurse called me to her office, wondering what I had done wrong now.

"Oh, yes, Miss Still," and she rummaged through papers on her desk. "Your transfer orders came in this morning."

"Oh, really?" and I sat down abruptly on the edge of a chair and watched apprehensively as she picked up three or four pages stapled together.

"I'm rather surprised at this," she said at last. "There are usually so many requests for overseas duty."

"Overseas," I practically shouted. I had never been out of the States, much less California, and as I looked at the documents in my trembling hands, I skipped the details and focused on the "where":

. . . YOU ARE HEREBY ORDERED TO REPORT TO THE COMMANDANT OF THE 16TH NAVAL DISTRICT, CAVITE, P.I. FOR ACTIVE DUTY AT THE U.S. NAVAL HOSPITAL, CAÑACAO, P.I. ON OR ABOUT 1 FEBRUARY 1940.

"Oh, my goodness! Where is Cañacao, P.I.?"

"That, my dear girl, is just about as far away as the Navy is likely to send you. Cañacao is next to the Cavite Navy Yard, at the south end of Manila Bay. The Philippine Islands are about halfway between China and Australia. Check the world globe in the Nurses Quarters. It's way out there in the Pacific. Way beyond the International Date Line."

I was homesick even before I began to pack. With mixed feelings, I took a last look at this pink mission-styled institution, so close to the fabulous Balboa Park, perched atop the green rolling hills that overlooked the harbor's Navy base, but like my three friends before me, I would soon be off to new and distant lands.

While I was home in Long Beach during my two weeks' vacation, I went to the local public library to read about the Philippine Islands, the American Commonwealth where I would spend my next tour of duty. I learned much of the fascinating, war-torn history and of the country's struggle for independence, from the 1898 Spanish-American War to the present problems between President Emanuel Quezon and Major General Douglas MacArthur, son of the late General Arthur MacArthur.

Of particular interest to me would be the ongoing tension between the ruling-class caciques and the downtrodden taos, at whose expense the former had built their wealth. Later I would be interned at Los Baños in barracks built by the taos.

"Be sure to take a long party dress," I was told, and I spent more than I could afford to buy one. True, the Navy would reimburse me for transportation, but I had to borrow money from my aunt to buy a train ticket to San Francisco. "Pay me with some nicely embroidered Chinese linens," she said.

My sister Paula (with her infant son) and our parents came to the Los Angeles railroad station to see me off. My brother-in-law, David, had to go to work, but he left a note: "Have a good time, Dixie."

"Tell him I intend to," I told Paula, and as the train pulled out of the station, tears were streaming down Mother's cheeks.

2

ARRIVAL IN FANTASYLAND

Whitecaps sparkled under a January icy blue sky as a brisk wind swept across San Francisco Bay. The salty air, fresh tar, fishy odors, the sights and sounds of a busy harbor were familiar enough, but this time I was not a spectator.

The *Henderson* was tied to one of the many piers along the Embarcadero. Departure time was drawing near. The ship's turbines had been rumbling for hours. It shuddered spasmodically as billows of smoke poured from its single stack, its exhaust churning the water behind it. A chugging tugboat stood by.

My roommate, Velda Forsyth, and I shivered more from excitement than cold as we leaned on the top deck railing to watch the last-minute hustle and bustle below. We both laughed when two China-bound second lieutenants came marching smartly across the pier as if they were a part of their 4th Marine Regiment on parade. In unison, they made a sharp right turn, clicked their heels, gave us a snappy salute, broke rank, and ran up the gangway. There they offered another snappy salute to the ship's flag and then to the officer of the deck, who granted them permission to come aboard.

Velda and I had met Sam Blair and Maury Randall the previous evening at the local officers club, and what a great time we'd had. With three good friends aboard, this promised to be an exciting trip.

At last an ear-splitting blast came from the ship's foghorn. A bosun's mate piped attention with "Now hear this. All ashore that's going ashore."

Lucille Redecker was among the late arrivals. Fashionably dressed, the slim, matronly woman was accompanied by three Navy nurses who, in their white uniforms, Navy sweaters, and long red-lined capes, hurried with her over to the gangway.

Then the gangway came aboard and dock hands slipped the mooring lines over the stanchions. After the tugboat nosed the *Henderson* out and away, the ship's foghorn seemed to say "Thanks" in response to its little helper's friendly toots.

We soon got underway and Sam and Maury came up to the top deck. They joined us in the bow's sheltered area, from where we took in the panorama of the busy Embarcadero and San Francisco's skyline. Along with everyone else, we watched the Golden Gate Bridge approach, magnificent with its bright red paint against the blue sky.

"San Francisco will be celebrating the bridge's third anniversary in a few days," Velda said.

"That's news to me," I said. Taking my cold hands in his, Sam said, "You're a Californian, and you didn't know that?"

But Velda knew all about it, right down to the last bolt. What a photographic memory!

"God, what an awesome feat of engineering," Maury said, gazing upward at its towers and the intricate cables that supported the road decking. "Marvelous! Absolutely marvelous!"

The bridge was equally spectacular from the west side, but while everyone else was admiring it, I felt sick with misgivings. Through the misty windows, all I could see was my mother, my sister, and my father waving good-bye at the Los Angeles railroad station. I had never been farther than a phone call away, and again, as in leaving the San Diego Naval Hospital, I felt an over-whelming homesickness.

"Hang on!" someone yelled. "We're heading into some rough water!" And from up here, we could see huge swells engulf the bow of the ship as it seemed to twist from side to side. Up the water came, gushing from stem to stern, and this continued until we were out into the open sea.

Five days later, aloha chimes from Pearl City's tower greeted us. Ukulele-strumming Hawaiians accompanied graceful girls dancing the hula-hula. Swaying grass skirts and graceful hand motions unmistakenly told a welcome story.

As soon as the gangway was down, up came other Hawaiian girls loaded with leis, each passenger receiving at least one with a friendly kiss. Then I heard "Dottie! Dottie!" and there were my three friends from San Diego, Adelma, Hazel, and Bonnie.

Everyone aboard seemed to know someone here, and for the next few days, I hardly saw any of the passengers, not even Velda. Tours around Oahu were ever so exciting with so many beautiful sights to see. I had my first frog's legs at a restaurant with Adelma, had dinner with Bonnie on the hospital ship *Relief* anchored there in Pearl Harbor with so many warships close by, and toured the hospital with Hazel. But all too soon, it was time to leave.

"Toss your leis overboard as you pass Diamond Head," we were told. "If they float back to shore, you will return someday."

This we did, and watched them float back to shore. "Oh, Dottie, I hope we can stay longer when we come back," Velda said.

Miss Redecker was popular with the passengers, many of them old friends. Velda and I alternately stood by for sick call, not that we were called upon very often. There was always something to do — play volleyball under a huge net on the top deck, dance to the nickelodeon in the officers recreation room, play cards, listen to the radio, or just visit.

Radio news about the war in Europe was not

nearly as interesting as the soothing voice of President Franklin Delano Roosevelt, who had been nominated for a third term. He had the Democrats' support because he brought the nation out of the Depression, but to the Republicans, the Pacifists, and the Isolationists, he was a warmonger.

Passing the International Date Line, we uninitiated travelers earned a Neptune Certificate. Thank goodness we weren't subjected to the humiliating practices of the 1800s. Instead, on a stage set up topside, the two Marines, Velda, and I attempted to sing a quartet, but no one could hear us.

"It's a good thing you girls were wearing long gowns!"

"It's a good thing you guys were hanging onto us, or our skirts could have blown right over our heads!"

Next was Guam, and Miss Redecker went ashore with the other passengers reporting in here. "As you know, my dears," she said, "with measles aboard, the ship is quarantined. I wish you better luck on your trip back. Guam is so small that we nurses customarily spend one year of our tour here, and the second one in the Philippines. I will see you then?"

We would indeed see her then, and we would spend more time with her than we thought.

At last the *Henderson* entered the San Bernardino Strait, the center of the 1,000-mile-long Philippine archipelago. One of the ship's officers pointed out Samar Island on our left as we passed it, and farther west was the tail end of Luzon on the right. He named visible islands on the ship's course through the Sibuyan Sea, the good-sized Mindoro south of the Verde Island Passage, and on we sailed into the South China Sea.

By the time we approached the breakwater in Manila's Port Area, the ship's executive officer had given Velda and me a rundown on what our new station was like.

"No, that's not a battleship," he said of a rock island on the right as the ship approached the entrance to Manila Bay. "It's the Army's Fort Drum. That's the superstructure of the battleship *Idaho*, scuttled after the last big war. It's manned by soldiers dressed like sailors and they carry on as though it really were a Navy ship.

"That volcanic rock island on our left is Corregidor, another Army fort, but a regiment of the 4th Marines uses Monkey Point. It's on the tail end of this polliwog-shaped island."

The Navy base was in the Cavite Province, in Manila Bay's southeast section. It was at the tip of a long slender peninsula, the tip resembling a lobster's claw forming Cañacao Bay. The hospital compound, on the west side, faced the Navy Yard on its causeway-connected island. Beyond this was huge Bacoor Bay, whose shores lined most of Manila Bay's east side.

Between San Roque and San Antonio was the Pan American Airline base, and the officer told us that whenever its transoceanic flying boat, the

China Clipper, came in or left, it taxied in front of the hospital compound. Anxiously checking his watch, he rattled off, "Inside the Sangley Point Gate are family quarters, a little schoolhouse, a warrant officers club, an officers club, Pat Wing 10 with its PBYs, and that's about all I have time to tell you."

In the breakwater, the ship inched along so slowly that it made no wake whatever before a tugboat finally pushed it alongside Pier 7.

Pearl of the Orient, so Manila's chamber of commerce said, but I couldn't say it had Hawaii's luscious green topography or its friendly, carefree charm. It had a personality of its own with a mixture of modern American and centuries-old Spanish architecture. Palms and barren flame trees lined the stretch of Dewey Boulevard on the parklike waterfront ahead of nicely designed plazas and hotels, and I could see a high diving board over a windbreaker wall ahead of the Army and Navy Club. Between the club and the famous Manila Hotel was the expansive, landscaped Luneta with its walkways and benches. Between the hotel and Pier 7 was the Lagaspi Landing, where the *San Felipe* ferry took passengers to and from Cavite.

A six-passenger Navy station wagon was waiting on the pier for those of us headed for Cavite, and I for one wasn't ready for this. "Manila's crowning disgrace" were the calesas that must have come over with the Spaniards. These black fringe-topped carts were drawn by frightened blinder-wearing ponies who were little taller than the two slender four-foot wheels. Heavyweight passengers could lift the poor little ponies right off the ground, and how awful to see their masters beat them so unmercifully.

Right-hand-drive vehicles meant getting accustomed to going down the left side of the road, and as if this wasn't bad enough, the noisy Filipino drivers must have thought horns were as essential as gasoline.

"Our driver says he'll take us through the old Walled City," Chief Petty Officer Roberts said, "if there are no objections."

We entered through the Santa Luna Gate, whose archway was in a high ivy-covered wall that must have been better than five feet thick. This was the original Spanish fort, the driver said. It still had its old prison bordering the Pasig River. A tourist trap, with its dark, dank dungeons. Here, so the story went, prisoners were drowned by high tides that washed them out into the bay.

U.S. Army signs seemed to be everywhere. Among an impressive bumper crop of Catholic churches were well-kept homes and shops. Our driver pointed out the Navy Dispensary, the only Navy structure here, before driving on through the Victoria Gate, onto Taft Avenue and into Manila's congested and noisy business district.

Beyond this the traffic thinned out as we rode eastward through a newer section of town. In the Ermita district we passed the sprawling Philippine University campus that included schools of medicine, veterinary sciences, and chemical engineering and government laboratories. Santa Scholastica, where we would later be prisoners, was in the next district, the elite Malate district.

Once outside the city limits, the wide paved avenue narrowed to a two-lane macadam road that more or less skirted the bay's shoreline. Here everything changed from ultra-modern to quaint to semiprimitive. All along the thirty-mile drive, we passed through villages and barrios whose thatch nipa shacks were built on bamboo poles, all made with dried palm leaves and/or rushes. Some stood so dangerously close to the road that we hung on for dear life, especially when it didn't seem there would be enough room for us and the overloaded open buses and cars coming from the opposite direction. Equally threatening were the ferocious-looking long-horned carabaos ambling along with unconcerned Filipinos astride them.

There were artesian wells and drainage ditches where native women washed both dishes and clothes. Bare-bottomed children and livestock splashed in the water at will. Singer sewing machines seemed out of place in many of the shacks' open windows, but most bizarre was a marching jazz band playing "Roll Out The Barrel." It was not a parade but a funeral procession, and joyous celebrants followed an elaborate hearse.

At last we checked in at the Navy Yard's Commandancia. Once these formalities were accomplished we got another ride, this time through San Antonio, into the Cañacao Reservation, and through the Cañacao Naval Hospital's gate.

The hospital's spacious compound was impressive, with its arcade of scattered mahogany trees and tropical plants. From the gate, a road encircled the hospital. Behind it was the fire station, laundry, water tower, warehouse, garage, morgue, a bowling alley, and an old Spanish cistern bearing the Philippine Historical Society's bronze marker. Like a windowless Quonset hut, this thick-walled structure was a part of the Spanish Navy's hospital run by a Catholic nursing order. Now it was used as a storeroom.

Between the front of the hospital and the seawall were bungalows for the senior doctors and their families, the skipper's residence several yards away from a walkway that connected the road to the *San Felipe* ferry landing. The first building inside the gate housed the Bachelor Officers Quarters, and our Nurses Quarters, a good-sized city block beyond the hospital, were halfway between the Corpsmen Quarters and the seawall.

We had a two-storied building designed for gracious living with wide, screened-in verandas on both airy floors where we led a pampered life. Filipino houseboys burnished the mahogany floors and woodwork until they were as shiny as the brass doorknobs themselves. We had only to set our shoes outside our doors to have them cleaned and polished. Maids washed and ironed our clothes, made our beds, and kept our rooms neat and clean. Best of all, old expressionless Marciano, a chef "excellencia," never failed to stock the refrigerator with an ample supply of luscious midnight snacks.

What a delightful setting by day, one that became a fantasyland in the colorful twilight hours, and pure magic under the thousands of stars in the night sky. Miniature lighthouses along the seawall glowed like amber gems, and reflections from the Navy Yard's lights danced across the surface of the water. Who could have asked for anything more romantic than this in the moonlight?

I was so fascinated by the historical setting here that, with the commanding officer's permission, I spent hours going through the hospital's archives with its intriguing old records. Inspired, I bought a cute little Underwood typewriter with its special *n* tilde key for Spanish names. I learned that since the days of the carabao-drawn narrow-gauge railway that ran by what had been the Spanish Navy's hospital, there had been ever so many changes before this modernized compound had been built.

Formals and party dresses were an absolute must, and when I could afford it, I trod the beaten path to Josie's dress shop in Manila. It was a happy and relaxed duty station, where "Nothing gets done on Mondays, ma'am. On Wednesdays, we make a fore 'n aft sweepdown for a white-glove inspection on Thursdays, and on Fridays, everybody's getting ready for another weekend liberty. And so you see, ma'am, the only time anything gets done around here is on Tuesdays."

Sometimes we made reservations for one of the Navy Yard's station wagons to take us on tours. We admired the highly polished figurines and wood salad plates and serving bowls at Tinio's and wandered around the Chinese cemetery, where, in raised coffins, masked faces of the deceased looked at us through glass windows. Respectful relatives left food at many of the graves.

Aguinaldo's Department Store carried Stateside items not available in the Ships Service inventory, and among the Manila Trading Center's treasures were wooden-soled bakias, shower shoes, with straps cut from inner tubes. Filipino merchants even visited our Nurses Quarters with all sorts of irresistible items, but with 140 pesos a month (70 American dollars) I had to be choosy.

Days sped by. Oh, how I loved to stand next to my special little lighthouse on the seawall, the farthest one down. Shivers ran up and down my spine when I watched Pat Wing 10's PBYs roar overhead in V-formation, and I almost felt the gigantic spray of water when they touched down.

I could see tops of ships when they were in the drydock just beyond the hospital compound, and in Cañacao Bay, I saw ships anchored and others tied up in the Navy Yard, bustling with its towers, cranes, and warehouses. The old Spanish building that once housed Spanish seamen was now a supply depot, and few were aware that beneath the Yard's tennis courts was a well-stocked ammunition dump with enough explosives to blow the little island and the surrounding area to smithereens.

But little did I know how obsolete the Asiatic fleet really was.

3

HAPPY DAYS

Sam wasn't much of a correspondent, but Maury sent very interesting letters. He was stationed at the American sector of the International Settlement in Shanghai, but only the American and Japanese sectors were fully staffed. With the upheaval in Europe, the English had sent most of their ships and personnel to Singapore on the Malay Peninsula, and the French had sent theirs south, somewhere along the Indochina coast. The Japanese soldiers were apparently positively rude and insulting to those remaining in their settlements.

I was surprised to learn that the Asiatic fleet's kingpin was not the admiral in the Navy Yard. Admiral Thomas C. Hart was the fleet's commander in chief, and according to Maury, he and his family spent the winter months in Manila. If his flagship *Augusta* was anchored in Manila Bay, I wasn't aware of it.

As for "Tommy" Hart, Maury said he came to the Settlement early in 1939 to spend his final years in the Navy before his retirement at age sixty-two. He said the admiral made periodic trips to Tsingtao, where Sam's regiment was part of the American Embassy, and this was Maury's chance to keep in touch.

I was also surprised to hear that except for the flagship and the light cruiser *Marblehead* in Tsingtao, there wasn't much more out there than a submarine, a dozen destroyers, riverboats, barges, and a few other auxiliary vessels.

In closing his letters, Maury would always say that he and Sam were looking forward to seeing Velda and me when we made the loop on either the *Henderson* or the *Chaumont*, which came out alternately. But we never did see them.

Our pleasant life at the hospital went on, and outgoing nurses were replaced by Julia O'Neal and Joyce Alcott, who came out on the *Chaumont*. With her blond boyish-bobbed hair and ready smile, Julia was a happy sort of person who made you feel good about yourself. Joyce, who had a unique personality of her own, had a boyish figure and beautiful long red hair, which she braided and wrapped artistically around her head.

With this exchange of personnel, I was overjoyed when our chief nurse, Miss Purvis, gave me permission to move into the back corner room. From the veranda I could practically touch the fascinating many-trunked banyon tree whose branches rerooted in the ground. After dark I could see the reflection of the lights from the Navy Yard and the amber lights along the seawall. When it was quiet, I could hear the water slapping against the seawall.

Velda and I had become good friends on the *Henderson*, and I now barely noticed her peculiarities. Going somewhere with her meant waiting until she found a safety pin to replace a lost button or hold a seam together, and she couldn't always remember to put her clothes out for the maids to clean and press. Her rundown heels had a low priority. Hairpins were always falling out of her fine sandy hair, and she was always pinning it up again. Sports was not one of her strong points. On the golf course, when she dubbed or missed the ball completely, she would pout and scold herself, but with her lively spirit and sense of humor, she was a source of entertainment in herself.

Captain Roth replaced our commanding officer. At the change-of-command ceremony we all were duly impressed with his impatient foot-tapping attitude as he seemed to look down his nose at us. On the wards he could be heard long before he could be seen, but we relaxed somewhat when we discovered that his bark was worse than his bite.

On its July trip, the *Henderson* brought Ellen Cunningham and Harriet MacLean. Ellen's brown eyes looked as though she used eye shadow (which we didn't have back then). She was a gentle, mousy sort of nurse who was so soft-spoken that one had to pay close attention to understand what she was saying.

"Speak up!" Harriet would yell, but she and

Ellen had already formed a solid friendship during their long ocean trip together, and Ellen was not offended. Harriet, with her curly auburn hair, came from Pennsylvania, and soon the corpsmen were teasing her about that, as they liked to tease us nurses about everything. Pharmacist's Mate 3c Casey Jones called Harriet "the coal miner's daughter."

Like the captain, the Irish lass could be heard long before she was seen, and Miss Efficiency did indeed run a tight ship. Taking over a ward where she'd left off was always a pleasure.

The *Henderson*'s next trip came in on schedule, and Miss Redecker replaced dear Miss Purvis. She wasn't the same as she had been on the ship, and she now kept a margin of distance between herself and those under her command. Her icy hazel eyes could say as much as her softly spoken words through clenched teeth. She visibly set a good example for the Nurse Corps, with her ladylike manner, her head held high, and her pinned-up black hair always as neat as the stylish clothes she wore.

The *Chaumont*'s next trip brought dietitian Bobbie Anderson and Olga Sturges. I liked Bobbie, with her subtle sense of humor. She was a nice-looking woman, but I didn't think she got out in the sunshine as much as she ought to. Olga had a nice smile when she chose to use it, but it was soon clear that I would not likely be one of her best friends.

"My word, Olga," I would tease her, "if I didn't

eat any more than you do, I'd collapse!"

"That's because you're so *tall* and *athletic*," she said, as though my five feet, six and a half inches were monstrous, and athletics were unladylike. But, I reminded myself, this was a first impression, and first impressions don't always mean much.

In October 1940, Maury wrote me that because relations between the Japanese and the other sectors of the Settlement had deteriorated so noticeably, Admiral Hart had ordered Navy dependents to return to the States. Maury thought dependents in the Philippines would probably be on their way out as well, but this wasn't something that could happen overnight. Nevertheless, by about mid-February 1941, the nurses were the only women left on the Navy base.

Maury wrote me that Admiral Hart was going to spend the cold winter months in the Philippines. Not only that, he was moving his headquarters to Manila, this time on the heavy cruiser *Houston*, which replaced his former flagship. The Marines in Shanghai and Tsingtao were to remain until ordered out, and Maury said he wouldn't be surprised if the Japanese were up to something.

With the admiral came the *Marblehead*, the destroyers from up there, the submarine from Tsingtao, and a few barges and auxiliary ships. Now that he was in Manila, Hart moved his headquarters from the *Houston* to Pier 7 and resided in the Manila Hotel as he had on previous sojourns. It wasn't long before Navy officers at the clubs were complaining about how old "Sundowner" Hart couldn't find anything good to say about their ships. He didn't like the lackadaisical attitude of the personnel, and he wanted all the ships thoroughly overhauled, *right now*. Old Sundowner insisted on drills, drills, and more drills, not only on the ships but at Sangley Point as well.

Before long the Yard's admiral was a patient; on top of all this stress, his son met with an accidental death.

By springtime 1941 a squadron of PBYs had arrived from Pearl Harbor, and those of us who played golf on Sangley Point's nine-hole golf course soon ran into their pilots.

It was over a few San Miguel beers at the tenth hole that I met Ensign Johnny Osbourne. He was lamenting the fact that instead of flying PBYs with the rest of the gang, he would fly one of the two bi-wing scouting floatplanes on the "USS No Sail."

He was talking about the *Langley*, of course, the old tub that "was stuck in coffee grounds so long it couldn't move if it wanted to." I had heard that said often, but when they started to tease, saying it was the most heavily armed ship in the Navy, I protested. I'd seen movies on its half flight deck and I'd had dinner in its officers mess, and I certainly hadn't seen armament of any kind on it. Finally line officer Ensign Jake Hanson gave me the lowdown.

In World War I it had apparently been the coal carrier *Jupiter*, and in the years to follow, it had been converted into an experimental aircraft carrier. It was named in honor of Professor Samuel P. Langley, the aviation pioneer, who conceived the idea, and the Navy's first aircraft carrier came to life. During the conversion, the weight of the flight deck seems to have become so heavy that the ship began to list, and to give it ballast, tons of World War I artillery and cannons were encased in cement in the bottom of its hull. After it had served its purpose, half the flight deck was removed, and it was shipped out here to serve as a tender for the PBYs. When I asked how the two-seater bi-wing scouting planes took off and got back on, Johnny said the derrick on the port side lowered them into the water and then hauled them back up.

"But right now, chick, you are going to dance with me." Grabbing my arm, this tall sandy-haired fellow ushered me to the nickelodeon, where he made his selection: "Oh, Johnny, Oh, Johnny, How You Can Love." What a conceited guy!

Johnny had never been assigned to a ship's crew before. Now, much to his annoyance, he stood watch along with the other junior line officers, and although the Langley seldom left the dock, its skipper stuck by old Sundowner's orders to drill, drill, and drill some more.

In any event, I began to see more of Johnny, self-satisfied soul that he was, and less of other dates as he made himself something of a fixture in the Nurses Quarters, and I really enjoyed his company. It was fun to have dinner with him at the Army and Navy Club in Manila, or dine and dance at the Jai Alai Club.

"*That,* chick, is the *Houston.* Isn't it a beaut?" he said as we passed it on the *San Felipe* ferry, and it was indeed. The sleek cruiser, two football fields long, was quite an awesome sight. As an aviation cadet, Johnny had seen this ship under construction during the disarmament period, and although designed as a heavy cruiser, it was light-weight when it was new. He'd toured it once, and he told me all about the special elevator that was installed to accommodate President Roosevelt's wheelchair when he took short cruises on it. It had a colorful history, but all that remained now were a few of the many gifts bestowed upon it by the proud city of Houston where it was chris-tened. Now wartime armor plates lined its hull.

"Those are the same scouting planes I'm flying now," Johnny told me more than once. "One of these days I'll be hitting the blue from that cata-pult!"

Not likely, I thought, but there were times when I wished he would, especially when he and his friends had too much to drink. Someone in-variably would take a friendly jab at someone else or make a provoking remark, fists would fly, and the dimwits would be having a great time. Then came the day when their opponents were the submariners from the four new *Sea* series subs, and Johnny ran into a haymaker that sent him sprawling.

It serves you right, I thought, and walked home in disgust.

But I couldn't stay mad for long. Time and again I asked him to call before he came over, but there he would be in the living room when I came off duty.

"Hey, come here, chick. Listen to this." And he'd tell me another story that soon had us both laughing ourselves silly.

Between outings with Johnny, I got to know the Navy Yard's admiral, who became one of my favorite patients. He was being "invalided home" because of what Admiral Hart called "chronic colds and indigestion," and flight arrangements to send him out on the *China Clipper* came on short notice. He was to leave early on Sunday, and he excitedly told me he wanted to give a cocktail party for the doctors and nurses at the Commandancia.

"You are to organize it, you hear? We have only Wednesday, Thursday, and Friday to choose from. What day shall it be?"

"Admiral, I'd better get permission from Miss Redecker," but no, there was no time for that. He had talked about his involvement in the *Langley*'s conversion into "the Covered Wagon," and since Johnny's name had come up related to

41

this, he was to be invited.

"As far as I know, Admiral, he has the OD watch on Wednesday and Thursday evenings." The date was set for Friday.

I discovered that the only way not to accept an admiral's invitation to a party was to drop dead when I learned that both Captain Roth and Miss Redecker had made other plans, and both were furious. To make matters worse, the admiral told me he would send a car over that afternoon so that I could go make arrangements with his household staff, and who should answer the door when the car showed up? Miss Redecker! And there was the admiral's empty limousine waiting for me.

Oh, it was a good party all right. Everyone had a great time, especially the admiral and Johnny. That is, everyone except Captain Roth, Miss Redecker, and me.

1941's summer turned into autumn, the *Langley* broke loose from its bed of coffee grounds to take part in the maneuvers, and the Cañacao hospital was in a state of panic. Enlisted patients with poliomyelitis came in from Sangley Point in what seemed to be the makings of an epidemic. Fortunately that didn't materialize, yet all the afflicted patients were desperately ill. Some were luckier than others, but Jeffery Morse, paralyzed from his neck down, had to be put into an iron lung.

There were too many of them for our little

two-room isolation unit, and the former school-house had to do. Day and night the same corpsmen were confined with them during the infectious stage, and Harriet, Dr. Kleinfeldt, and Dr. Mahoney also played active roles. The rest of the staff watched anxiously until this contagious siege was over.

Then we had to take the polio patients out of the contaminated area and into a clean ward, which was a tedious task, especially moving the iron lung. This had to be cleaned to my satisfaction, and then the corpsmen had to manually operate it while it was being brought into the 75-bed ward and placed where it could be seen from the ward's office window.

"Miss Still, ma'am, I'd like to have the bed next to the iron lung," another patient said as we worked.

"What an unusual request, Donaldson, it's so noisy."

"Yes, ma'am, but I've been sleeping next to it all along. That's my buddy in there, and I wake up the minute anything goes wrong."

What a fine gesture, I thought later, back at the Nurses Quarters. I took my cap off and ran my fingers through my hair, exhausted. A letter from Paula was on the entry hall table, and I put it in my pocket to read later.

"Johnny! For heaven's sake, you scared the daylights out of me!"

"Hey, chick, do you see anything different?"

"Oh, I don't know, you're wearing your khaki

uniform, and other than buttons that are about to pop off, no."

"You're sure you don't see *anything* different?" He shifted his shoulders around as if to call attention to the insignia on his collar.

"Well, congratulations, Lieutenant Junior Grade Johnny Osbourne!"

"And you know what else?"

"What else, Lieutenant?"

"I'm being transferred to the *Houston*! To the U-S-S *HOUSTON*!"

"You don't mean it! Oh, how wonderful!"

From his pocket came an attractive necklace. "This is for that new formal you've been talking about. We are going to celebrate!"

Later that night, in the Manila Hotel's dimly lit ballroom, waltzing in his arms as the vocalist sang, "Let Me Call You Sweetheart," I was deliciously happy. Looking up into his laughing eyes, I felt as pretty as I'm sure I must have looked, as proud as he was of the stripe and a half on his neatly pressed dress uniform, so thrilled about his advancement and transfer to the *Houston*.

4

PEARL HARBOR

By the beginning of November 1941, Captain Boyle had replaced Captain Roth, Captain Putnam had replaced the executive officer, and Commander Walters, a grumpy perfectionist, I thought, had replaced the hospital's chief surgeon. Three nurses were also replaced.

We now had Sarah Brent, an experienced nurse-anesthetist, a history and current-events buff of sorts who seemed to be smoking cigarettes incessantly except when on duty; Elizabeth Moran; and Amy Aldrich. Both of the latter were coming from Guam, and with a two-week vacation coming up, both were on their way to the Army's Camp John Hay resort in Baguio. Neither was taller than five-foot-two at best, and it seemed to me it wouldn't take much of a breeze to blow them away.

"You girls should have eaten more spinach when you were growing up," I told them.

"I can't stand the stuff!" Liz said, and Amy smiled evasively.

Liz, like Harriet MacLean, was an outgoing chatterbox. She was the youngest of a large family in Philadelphia, but the only things the two nurses had in common was their Irish heritage, the state of Pennsylvania, and curly auburn hair. They had not known one another before becoming a part of the Navy Nurse Corps, nor were they destined to become the best of friends.

Amy had grown up in a town not far out of Los Angeles. She was a good and thoughtful nurse, but so shy that she backed off from any social events that involved mixed company. Whenever we had male dinner guests, she left the dining room as soon as she could politely do so.

Now that Johnny was attached to the *Houston*, his sense of importance climbed several more notches. A date with him usually included his tagalong shipmates, and this evening at the Jai Alai Club was no exception. He, like the others, had had too much to drink, and involved in their noisy and ridiculous behavior, he seemed to have forgotten I was there. To heck with them, I thought, and I decided to enjoy the company of the *Langley*'s line officers. Dancing with one of them, I noticed that Jake was sitting at the table where Johnny, another drink in hand, apparently was taking a breather. When we got closer, I heard Jake say, "There's going to be a war, sure as hell. Marry her, Johnny, and send her back to the States before it's too late."

Johnny laughed! I couldn't believe it, but he actually laughed as if that was a big joke! Hurt and angry, I picked up my wrap, hailed a taxi, and reached the Lagaspi Landing in time to catch the *San Felipe*'s last run to Cañacao.

To get married before my transfer orders came in was unthinkable anyway: I would be sent home. But while I was doodling with "Lt. j.g. and Mrs. John Osbourne" and "Mrs. Dorothy Osbourne," it turned out he had no intention of marrying me at all!

From the Cañacao dock, I kicked twigs and anything else in my path on the way to my little lighthouse, where I couldn't keep the tears back. After a while, the rhythmic sound of the water gently slapping the seawall was like a soothing lullaby. Lights from the Navy Yard still danced on the water; stars still twinkled in the sky. It was peaceful here. As for you, Johnny, I don't ever want to see you again! Not ever! Furthermore, I won't be at home when you call!

But Johnny couldn't have called even if he had wanted to. Long before the crack of dawn, Navy Yard mechanics were pulled off the *Houston* so unexpectedly that unfinished jobs had to be completed while the ship was in motion. Its white paint was still being covered with a battleship gray as it steamed out of Manila Bay, and by the time my alarm clock sounded off, the Asiatic fleet was sailing southward.

Whenever the fleet was out on maneuvers, the base's boisterous fun and laughter went with it. Sunday evenings were notoriously dull, but one particular Sunday was worse. We ordinarily chatty upstairs nurses were quietly and mechanically mending this or that, reading, pinning up hair, manicuring fingernails, or doing other mundane things.

On my desk, Johnny's letter had not one concerned word about my disappearance from the Jai Alai Club. Instead, he wrote about how he and the other officers had fought over a pair of binoculars to look at the half-naked native girls dancing on Bali's shores near the Equator. I hadn't intended to answer it, but having nothing better to do, I got as far as "6 December 1941" and "Dear Johnny."

With a sigh, I wandered aimlessly around the veranda. In the chilly salt air, palm fronds rattled quietly and moonlight filtering through the swaying branches of the mahogany trees created grotesque patterns on the ground. The moon's brilliance dimmed the streetlights and the glowing lighthouses. Reflections from the Navy Yard lights still danced, but there was nothing romantic about any of this. Shivering, I went back inside.

Dear Johnny, indeed! With a swish of my hand, his letter went flying into the wastebasket. Then, as if to punish him further, I kicked the wastebasket. Noting the pretty little bottle of cologne he gave me, I disdainfully picked it up from the dressing table and dropped it into the wastebasket. "I've got more to do with my life than mope about you!"

Oh, hell's bells! I can't stand this room another minute!

On went my shoes and socks, my Navy sweater and a windbreaker. Grabbing a scarf, I ran downstairs and out the front door. On the sidewalk I took a deep breath, tied the scarf over my head, and looked up into the moonlit sky. The red light blinked on the top of the nearby radio tower; a calesa pony clipclopped rhythmically as it pulled its cart toward the front gate. Its discharged passengers staggered happily toward the Corpsmen Quarters.

"Bell-bottomed trouser-er-er-z-z,
Coats of navy blu-oo-oo-hooo!"

"Shhh. Gotta be quiet," one of them cautioned, but soon they were singing as loudly as ever.

"Ooooh, the monkeys have no tails,
In Zam-boanga-a-a!"

They won't be much good tomorrow, I thought as I wandered over to sit next to my lighthouse. The chug-chug-chugging sound of the *San Felipe* coming around Sangley Point reminded me of the many times Johnny and I had come back on it, tired and happy.

Damn you, Johnny! You have become such a part of my life that everything reminds me of you! Songs we sang and danced to, Sangley Point, the Navy Yard, the officers clubs, Manila, even the Nurses Quarters itself! Damn you, Johnny! Damn you!

With its engines idling, the ferry glided by quietly, and I could see the Big Three getting ready to disembark. I knew what was coming next, but I still jumped at the roaring sound of its engines

49

being put into reverse.

That's enough to knock Captain Boyle out of his rocking chair, I thought. About the only things he and Captain Roth had in common were the four stripes on their shoulder bars and the gold braid on their hats. On Thursdays' white glove inspections, Captain Roth and his entourage would enter the wards with gusto and examine and comment about everything. Not Captain Boyle. All of a sudden there he was with Captain Putnam, and then they were gone, with not even so much as a pat on the back or a kick in the pants. No, it will never be the same now that Captain Roth has gone. Nothing will ever be the same, not that it matters. I'll be boarding the *Henderson*, going home the first of next month.

What a gloomy sight, I thought as I shifted my position and pulled my knees up inside the buttoned jacket. Except for those two submarines and a nest of four-stackers, all that's left are miscellaneous barges and whatnot. The Yard's as dead as a burned-out cigarette.

The *Sealion* and *Seadragon*, tied side by side next to a wharf, were undergoing an overhaul. I had run into several of their officers at the officers club or as dinner guests in our Nurses Quarters. Only last evening, Velda, Lizzy, Ellen, and I had accepted an invitation to dinner on the *Sealion*.

Hugging my knees and resting my chin on them, I thought about how I wouldn't have gone had Velda not talked me into it. I was glad she did: I had never been on a submarine before, and the efficient use of every inch of space was amazing.

"With such tight quarters as this," I asked, "whatever prompts such tall and athletic men as you to choose submarine duty?"

"Our wives ask that same question," was their laughing answer.

After an excellent dinner, the officers from both submarines escorted the four of us to the Army and Navy Club in Manila. Oh, such a fine group of men they were, so gentlemanly.

Getting colder, I tightened my scarf and pulled up my jacket collar. Pulling my hands up into the sleeves, I watched the Big Three come down the road.

Julia and Sarah waved amicably, but Miss Redecker's was more like a "get lost" wave, and I guessed I couldn't blame her. Ever since the admiral's party I definitely hadn't been her favorite nurse, but there was nothing I could do about that now.

Back in my room, I sat gloomily down at the desk. Damn you, Johnny! I fished his letter out of the wastebasket and tore it into little pieces. Then, impulsively, on my unfinished answer I wrote, YOU AND YOUR DAMNED HOUSTON CAN GO TO HELL! This went into an addressed envelope and over to the Administration Building. There at the Master-at-Arms' desk, I tucked it under some of the other letters in the outgoing box.

"Well, so much for you!" I said out loud just

before, snug in my bed, I dropped off to sleep.

As the bombs were falling on Pearl Harbor, on our side of the International Date Line it was around 0330 hours, 8 December 1941. The man on duty at the radio station picked up the frantic calls from 5,000 miles across the sea, and he called his commanding officer. He in turn called Admiral Hart, then his friend Bobbie here at the Nurses Quarters. She notified Miss Redecker.

By this time, Admiral Hart had already issued an order to all stations: "Japan has started hostilities. Govern yourselves accordingly." And, from his quarters in the Manila Hotel, he no doubt watched the lights in the entire Cavite Navy Base go out as the ships in Manila Bay became silhouettes in the waning moonlight.

Within minutes Miss Redecker and Julia were dressed. Armed with their blue cellophane-masked flashlights, they rushed over to the Administration Building to confer with the captain and the staff doctors. Dawn was still a few hours off when Joyce came back to the Nurses Quarters, and after setting up the big coffee pot, she rushed upstairs.

"Dottie, wake up!" she ordered. "No! Don't turn your light on! This is a blackout. Everyone is to get dressed in uniform and come downstairs immediately."

Joyce repeated this message as she hurried from one room to the next. This happened so fast that none of us were sure we had not imagined it, but

52

we all stumbled out into the dark hallway.

"Was that Joyce?"

"What's this about a blackout? Is that what she — ?"

"For heaven's sake, whose bright idea is it to have a drill in the middle of the night?"

"Hey, that's my foot you're stepping on!"

"Did Joyce say we're to get dressed and come downstairs?"

We watched ominous blue shadows bounce over the walls and ceiling as Joyce rushed up the stairwell with her masked flashlight.

"Joyce! What's going on?"

"Geez, back off, will ya? I've gotta get back to the hospital and I need my rosary! What's the matter with you all? How come you aren't getting dressed like I told you?"

We followed her as she rushed into her room. "At least you can tell us what's going on!"

Joyce ignored the chatter going on around her, and between a mumbled "geez" and a "gee whiz," she rummaged through her dresser drawers until she found a package of cigarettes, her lighter, and, finally, her rosary.

"Joyce, for heaven's sake, what's this all about? A drill at this hour?"

"Hell, no! This isn't a drill! The Japs are bombing Pearl Harbor!"

"You're kidding!"

"Oh, hell! My cigarettes. What did I do with my cigarettes?"

"They're in your pocket," Amy said.

War with the Japs? Yuk, that's all I need! Damn it, there goes my transfer orders!

Shivering thoughts of Bonnie, Hazel, and Adelma in Pearl Harbor flashed through my mind as I took out my flashlight, put in new batteries, masked it, and turned it on. Then, when I put the flashlight on the desk, it fell into the waste-basket.

Johnny! Oh, wow! I've got to get that letter back! Not that he doesn't deserve it, but this isn't the right time.

Dressed at last, I inspected my ghostly reflection in the mirror. Well, Lieutenant Johnny, I thought, you've been wanting to take a pot-shot at them, and I wish you luck! Hurrying downstairs, I thought if it really *is* a war, it can't last long. It can't be anything like the photos I've seen of Europe's battlefields in the last war. But, of course, we have to be prepared.

"You girls ready for a war?" Sarah asked with a smirk, her eyes squinting from her cigarette's smoke.

"No more than you are," Bobbie answered, and I chided Sarah about her lack of confidence in the Asiatic fleet.

She laughed, but I knew that our fleet could cope with whatever emergency might arise.

"Dear Gawd," Liz exclaimed, "wouldn't it be something if the Japs dropped a bomb on the hospital?"

"I knew I shouldn't have accepted orders for overseas duty," Amy murmured just as Miss Redecker and Julia came in.

"Ladies, I hardly know what to tell you. Captain Boyle has not yet been able to get instructions from the fleet surgeon. He could not get through to Admiral Hart's offices or the Commandancia. However, he did say that our ambulatory patients are to be discharged and sent back to duty as quickly as possible."

"You sure this isn't a drill?" Ellen asked quakingly.

"I wish it were, child. I only know there is much to be done and little time to do it. Please, ladies, do not dawdle."

At Miss Redecker's urging, we rushed out into the early dawn. Mud puddles left over from recent rains slowed us down somewhat, but we ran the full distance between the Nurses Quarters and the hospital.

"That took two minutes and twenty-three seconds," the pathologist announced, and reset his stopwatch.

No one lingered to argue the point.

5

MANILA UNDER ATTACK

Confusion reigned as the entire staff converged on the hospital. Too much time had lapsed since we'd been told what procedures to follow, and I couldn't exactly remember how, why, and what was to be done by whom. Most important to me was recovering Johnny's letter, but neither the outgoing nor incoming mailboxes were where I'd seen them last, nor could anyone at the Master-at-Arms' desk enlighten me. It would have to wait. "Baldwin, I want to hold a conference with all of you senior corpsmen," I said. "You probably know the ambulatory patients are to be sent back to duty." Yes, they knew that. "Dr. Mahoney will have to write discharge orders on those leaving." Probably so. "We are expected to have them ready to leave as quickly as possible, and I'm open for suggestions on the best way to accomplish this."

"No problem, ma'am. If they ambulate, they get discharged."

"Oh, honestly, Jones!" I said, threatening him with a fist.

"Careful, ma'am. I bruise easy."

Early morning care and breakfast went on despite all the confusion, but by the time Dr. Mahoney arrived we had tables and chairs set up in front of the nursing office. Ambulatory patients, charts in hand, waited to be seen, and by 1030 hours, discharge orders had been written for most of them.

"I'd like to be discharged, sir."

"Not now, Jackson. I want to go over the lab tests first."

"How do you feel, son? Think you're well enough to be discharged? You'll take your medications?" Yes, he would.

The retired Filipino mess attendant wanted to go home. "You're sure?" asked Dr. Mahoney. "We can send you over to the Veterans Hospital."

"Go home. Family need me."

It was no-go to a patient with an undetermined diagnosis; no-go to a man found to be diabetic. When all the no-go's had been sent back to their beds, the doctor made rounds for the others. At the end of the line, Jeffery Morse said, "I'd like to be discharged, sir."

"Sure thing, Jeff," Mahoney said affectionately.

"Too bad he wasn't out of the iron lung in time to get him out on the *Chaumont* with the others," I murmured.

"Baldwin! Where are you?" I yelled unprofessionally, sitting down at the desk, dreading the follow-up paperwork.

"Yes ma'am?"

57

"I need a messenger," I said, handing him the pack of prescriptions the doctor had ordered, "and here's a list of requisition forms I'll need. Who could *possibly* have more printed forms and red tape than the Navy? Another thing, Baldwin, we'll have to pull their personal belongings from the storeroom."

With the ward sounding more like a social event than a crisis, I looked at the stack of patients' charts and tried to make some sense of what was going on around me.

"Guess your boyfriend'll be knockin' the stuffin' outa them Japs," a patient said through the window.

"Oh, you betcha." Nosy, nosy. As nosy as the corpsmen.

A chief petty officer from the Yard brought in boxes of gas masks and helmets from the last war, and the hoopla and buffoonery going on didn't help one little bit. Before he left, the chief said everyone had to learn how to use the masks.

"Heard the California coast got blasted," someone said.

Ridiculous.

A fast-moving messenger from the Master-at-Arms' desk dropped a package of patients' mail on my desk. "Wait a minute! Is the outgoing mail still here?"

"Ma'am, I'm just an errand boy."

Half an hour later, Liz came in. "Honest to Gawd, Dottie, Miss Redecker doesn't know if she's coming or going. First she tells me to do this, then that, and now she sends me over here to help you out."

"Well, bless her cotton-pickin' heart! Here's the narcotics key. How about working with Berle in the treatment room? And Liz, maybe you could help Baldwin with the outgoing patients?"

Of course, neither of us could appreciate why our chief nurse had reason to be confused. The fleet surgeon had got permission to use the former dependents' ward at the Sternberg Hospital for our Navy patients temporarily. Then, with Captain Boyle and the executive officer, he'd tried unsuccessfully to find a suitable building in or around Manila that could be confiscated for the Cañacao Hospital. In the meantime, the medical officers here were too busy with other things, so it seemed, and thus Miss Redecker had fallen heir to a management task for which she was slightly better prepared than most of them.

"Heard the Japs wiped out the entire Pacific Fleet at Pearl," someone said.

Impossible!

An air-raid alert was heard. Before the question of what to do about it was resolved, the all-clear sounded, and the general consensus was that the Yard was trying out its equipment.

By noon, Filipino tuberculosis patients in the isolation unit were on their way to the Quezon Institution, and other supernumerary Filipino patients had gone home or been sent to the Veterans Hospital. Around fifty Navy and Marine Corps patients had been discharged from Ward C alone, leaving loads of unmade beds and piles of details yet to be taken care of.

"Leave it and come to lunch," Julia came by to say. "It'll be here when you get back."

We were all tired and glad to relax in the peaceful atmosphere of the Nurses Quarters, but as lunch was being served, we heard the mournful sound of the Yard's air-raid alert.

"Oh, dear, what are we to do?"

"What do you think the sandbags around the building are for?"

"Do you mean we are to go under the building and sit on the dirt in our uniforms?" Bobbie asked, and Miss Redecker said a substitute for our uniforms would be forthcoming.

Soon the all-clear sounded, and cases of sailors' dungarees and work shirts were delivered. Short-crotched men's pants, usually worn along the top of a sailor's pelvis, weren't made for curvaceous female figures, and the living room was filled with gales of laughter.

"Dear Gawd! I wouldn't be caught dead in one of them!" Liz said, and neither would the rest of us.

"The supply officer thought they might be useful," Miss Redecker said, "how could I turn him down?" She instructed each of us to to take four sets of pants and shirts, or more if we had room in our luggage. "Until we find something better, you may wear casual skirts and blouses, or suitable dresses."

With this settled, she went on, "Our remaining patients are to be transferred to Sternberg sometime tomorrow. A team of corpsmen, two doctors, and two of you nurses are to go with them. Would any of you care to volunteer?"

"I will," Ellen promptly said. "You will, too, won't you, Harriet?"

Harriet grimaced and said, "Why don't we draw straws?"

Good idea, and Julia said, "Harriet, I'll let you draw first." Harriet drew the short straw, and we all laughed uproariously until Miss Redecker reminded us that there were still urgent things to be done.

On the way back, Liz and I went over to the seawall to see what Dr. Mahoney and some of the ward corpsmen were looking at so intently.

"We're trying to figure out what's burning over there."

"Seems to be coming from somewhere near Parañagua."

"Maybe it's from Nichols Field. They could be burning off used oil."

The hospital was a mess, but our only recourse was to keep it in readiness until it could be moved. This meant replenishing supplies and putting the wards back in order. By the end of the day we all were dog-tired, and in the dining room, Miss Redecker explained what was going on as far as she knew.

"As you know, we are in a target zone and we

could be ordered out at a moment's notice. I strongly urge you to pack your personal belongings. It would be wise to pack a change of clothing and other immediate needs in a small suitcase."

This was good advice in more ways than one. It was something positive to do for ourselves, something to distract our anxious minds, and I'm sure it brought as many fond memories of wonderful days and happy times to the others as it did to me.

As I folded dresses bought in Josie's delightful dress shop, I could hear the proprietress gushing, "Dorothy, you are a perfect size fourteen. You should be a model. So tall and slender. I ordered this dress just for you." What a saleswoman!

Folding a print street dress, I thought of the wonderful times I'd had while wearing it. The last time was on a trip near the bat caves, and I could almost feel Johnny's arm draped casually over my shoulders as we stood next to his borrowed car. We watched the colors change with the setting sun, and when the last sliver of the sun vanished from the horizon, out came clouds and clouds of bats.

It also reminded me of an earlier eye-opening visit to an open-air market out in the countryside. It was a living example of the taos' plight I had read about. Strong whiffs of cheroots, the poor man's cigar, mingled nauseously with the stench of decaying slabs of meat, rotting fruits and vegetables, and open-pit latrines farther out. Nothing was clean in this poverty-stricken barrio, including the artesian well, but this seemed to have no effect on the natives' lively chatter and flashing smiles.

This dress reminded me of other dates and the pressure of unwanted invitations. But wanted or not, dates were always a battle against roaming hands, Johnny's included. Oh, Johnny, I wish I hadn't written that letter!

I took my favorite evening gown from its hanger and, just for a moment, I was waltzing blissfully with Johnny in the Manila Hotel's ballroom, lost in my own land of enchantment. I even started to hum the first few bars of "It Looks Like Rain in Cherry Blossom Lane."

"Here's your dictionary," Harriet said, dropping it on my desk.

"Thanks," I said, and in my dreamy world, I had no idea what she was saying as she rushed out.

I carefully folded the gown and put it on top of the others. Memories, wonderfully rich memories, went into the trunk. As advised, I had sent my Chinese chest, a nest of tables, and other treasures home on the last transport out, but there were still trinkets and other gifts Johnny had given me, each a reminder of some exciting place or event. All went into the trunk with my clothes, white uniforms, jewelry box, books, desk contents, and I needed six pairs of dungarees and work shirts to keep everything in place.

Tuesday started out on a calmer note; the unseemly festive air was gone. With fewer than 60 patients remaining throughout the 240-bed hospital, Ward C was eerie and foreboding with its echoing emptiness. Hushed voices among the few remaining patients clustered up front were uncanny, especially with the long rows of neatly made beds behind them.

"This is like being in the eye of a typhoon," Pharmacist Paul Phillips said as he leaned against the nursing-office doorjamb, wearily pushing his hat back to a jaunty angle on his curly red hair. "I'm looking for a few corpsmen to give me a hand. Got anybody you can spare?"

"Oh, I think so. My goodness, Mr. Phillips, you look so tired. Why don't you sit down for a spell and give me the latest scuttlebutt."

"Sure thing," he said, and his tall, lanky frame poured itself onto the chair next to the desk. Pulling his hat forward and tilting the chair backward so he could lean his head against the wall and close his eyes, he said, "Do you want to hear the good news or the bad news first?"

"Good."

He yawned. "Got a message for you from the *Houston*; a Pat Wing 10 officer called this morning." Another yawn. "Said he was sorry he couldn't deliver it himself." A pause and a stretch. "Had to leave on the double. I told him I'd be glad to oblige."

"Quit yawning and tell me what it is."

"Ah, it feels good to sit down. Didn't get much sleep last night." More yawning. "What a helluva time for a truck to get a flat tire."

"The message, Mr. Phillips?"

"Captain must think I'm superhuman," yawn, "and that I'm not." With both hands he rubbed his tired eyes.

"The message? If you *please?*"

The front legs of his chair hit the deck with a bang, and the next thing I knew, his face was right in front of mine. "He said his buddy sent you a kiss."

"Mister Phillips! For goodness' sake!"

"Well, it was worth a try," he said, settling back in his chair with a chuckle.

"Okay, okay. Now what's the bad news?"

"The bad news is I'm to finish getting the rest of the inventories in Stores and Ships Service packed and sent over to a bodega in Manila, and I'm bushed."

"I can see that, but may I buy a carton of cigarettes?"

"Let's make that compliments of the house. What brand do you want?"

If he isn't something, I thought, watching this freckle-faced warrant officer round up the corpsmen. He was one of their immediate Hospital Corps superiors, their teacher, and their friend. He had only to ask, and he had more volunteers than he needed.

It was lunchtime, and like the day before, the air raid's mournful wail interrupted our meal in the Nurses Quarters. This time the houseboys

65

brought mats for everyone to sit on in the dirt. By now the remaining patients were on their way to Sternberg, and, as we sat there, Miss Redecker asked us to prepare the hospital for whatever contingencies might arise.

"Captain Boyle expects to move the hospital out soon, but in the meantime we must not be caught short." The all-clear was heard.

Before the day was over, the empty hospital was in shipshape condition. Loads of bandages and dressings were wrapped, sterilized, and packed, ready to be used here or moved to Manila. Gallons of sterile distilled water and saline solutions were prepared. Every intravenous flask was filled and, come what may, we were ready for Miss Redecker's contingencies.

The next morning, 10 December, was unnervingly quiet. One or two patients came into the emergency room for minor injuries; that was all. In the Nurses Quarters at noon, we talked about the news reports on the radio that had little to offer, good or bad. The lead story in the morning's *Manila Tribune* asked that the citizens remain calm and not panic at the sound of the air-raid sirens. It also listed ways to protect oneself in event of an actual air raid.

"Here it says President Roosevelt made MacArthur a four-star general," Julia said, "and he is to lead the USAFFE. That's an acronym for the United States Armed Forces of the Far East. Huh? No, of course not. He won't be in charge of the Navy."

From our vantage point nothing was going on, yet vague apprehensions hung over us. The Navy Yard and Sangley Point gave a weak sense of security as we sat on pins and needles, and I wondered what exactly I should be so afraid of.

"I wouldn't be so scared if the fleet were here," Velda said.

"Don't worry," I said with an assurance that I didn't feel. "It'll be back before you know it." And, while the houseboys were serving Marciano's welcome lunch, there came another sad and mournful wail.

"No use leaving this," Julia said cheerfully. Following her lead, we all carried our lunches with us. Under the building, plates balanced on our laps, we put on a good front with our giggling and nervous quips.

"Geez, Japan is no bigger than my home state of South Dakota," Joyce said. "The damned Japs must be out of their minds, picking on Uncle Sam."

"Remember David and Goliath?" Sarah said, lighting a cigarette.

"We've been under here fifteen minutes already," Julia finally said. "Do you suppose they forgot to sound the all-clear?"

"Perhaps so," Miss Redecker answered, "but we had better wait a little longer."

In the disquieting atmosphere, the two houseboys were talking in their native Tagalog. The maids had already gone home, but —

"Lucille, where is Marciano?"

"Oh dear. He knows he should be down here."

"Ma'am, I go get him," one of the houseboys said.

"That sounds like an awful lot of airplanes!"

"Isn't that antiaircraft?"

"It's coming from the Yard!" So did the rapid sequences of BOOM! BOOM! BOOM!

We stopped talking as wave after wave of enemy bombers unhurriedly dropped their deadly cargo. Over the continuously exploding bombs, we heard fighter planes zooming over Sangley Point with their machine guns rat-a-tat-tatting. I knew Pat Wing 10 and the Navy Yard were knocking them down one after the other, and I shouldn't be so terrified.

A few feet away and next to a pillar, Olga was mouthing prayers as her fingers passed from one rosary bead to the next. Liz, head buried against her propped-up knees and hands trembling, was also saying the rosary. I could see how intensely Joyce was concentrating, her fingers stopping momentarily on each bead, and I envied these Catholic nurses who seemed to be getting so much comfort from their faith.

Religion had not been a part of my life, but oh, how I wanted to pray. What's the use, though, I thought. If God exists He won't listen to me. If anything bad happens to Johnny and the *Houston* it will be because I put a jinx on them, and dear Lord, don't let that happen. Oh, Johnny, I wish you were holding me in your arms. I'm so scared!

Minutes passed. Another five, ten, fifteen, and

the sounds of exploding bombs and roaring aircraft became so monotonous that unrelated thoughts drifted through my mind.

Joyce had said of Johnny, "Each to his own," but she should talk: her men friends weren't anything to boast about. Glancing at her, I could see she was still holding her rosary beads. What was she thinking about?

Bobbie isn't just pale, she's chalk white, and that's a mighty weak smile she's giving me. Come to think of it, I really don't know her any better than I know Liz or Amy. The way Amy's trembling, she must be pretty scared, too. And Velda. With her glasses off, I wonder if she can really see me. Guess so: she's trying to smile back at me. She's scared, they're all scared, so I guess it's okay for me to be scared too.

"There goes Marciano on my old bicycle," Joyce said.

"I'll bet the kitchen is clean and tidy and everything's been put away," Julia said.

My attention reverted to the constant bombing, and I shivered as I thought about the casualties that would be coming in. Japs, no doubt. At least we had plenty of sterile supplies.

Again my mind wandered in all directions as the forty-five minutes of bombing passed. Jarring sounds brought back the present momentarily, but the loud BOOM that shook the Nurses Quarters definitely brought me back to reality. Metal slammed against metal as the closest radio tower came down like a collapsible picnic cup, one section inside the next. Oh, God, don't let them hit this building! Don't let it fall down and bury us!

Deafening bombs exploded one after the other down Sangley Point's length, and the silence that followed was equally deafening. The enemy planes had expended their murderous load and flown away in the same tight formation as when they'd come.

"No point in waiting any longer," Miss Redecker said. As we came out from under the building, the horror of it all shocked us. The Navy Yard was flattened, and sporadic flames shot up through a blanket of black smoke. We dashed over to the hospital as fast as we could, and had the pathologist been out there with his stopwatch, he would have been flabbergasted!

6

THE YARD DESTROYED

Sometimes I try to imagine how Admiral Hart must have felt as he watched from the Marsman Building roof while his fleet's lifeline was being blasted out of existence. How helpless he must have felt, knowing that the Yard's antiaircraft guns couldn't reach them at that altitude. At least the ammunition dump on the Yard hadn't been hit and the radio station was still functional even though one of its wireless towers was down. Under his immediate command here in Manila Harbor he had only two destroyers, six PT boats, the submarine tender *Canopus*, which he ordered into shallow water, twenty-seven submarines, a salvage ship, three river gunboats, three minesweepers, and one tugboat. How disheartened he must have been, knowing he couldn't count on the Pacific Fleet to back him up.

Admiral Rockwell had probably also seen the Yard's well-aimed antiaircraft shells burst in black puffs well beneath their targets. It must have been a sickening sight, as bomb after bomb pulverized crucial equipment and installations. Black clouds everywhere obscured his view, but hatless, he ran out giving encouragement and first aid to casualties wherever possible. To his dismay, he learned that a direct hit killed all but one of the people in the dispensary. Dr. Kleinfeldt was hurled out into Cañacao Bay, but he managed to reach safety despite shrapnel injuries in his shoulder.

After the raid was over, the Yard's casualties joined the parade en route to the hospital while salvage and demolition operations took priority over the hundreds of unidentifiable human remains that would rot in the noonday sun for days awaiting interment in a common grave.

All of the Army's airports were wiped out on the first day of the war, and the Sternberg hospital was flooded with casualties who were placed, row after row, out on the front lawn. Each was given a quarter grain of morphine while an extensive triage was made to determine those most in need of immediate attention. That was impossible here. Roads from the Navy Yard were all but impassable, and hundreds of casualties — Filipinos, civilians, servicemen alike — came in on twisted corrugated roofing, splintered doors, dirty carpets, blankets, sawali mats, carabao carts, whatever happened to be handy. In the urgency of it all, they were dumped unceremoniously on the beds or on the floors in the wards and hallways. Some were already dead.

I was thunderstruck by what I saw on Ward C. The stench of burned flesh was as nauseating as

72

the sight of mangled humanity — oily, dirty, bleeding, agonizing. Arms and legs were broken at weird angles, some dangling by a shred, others with only jagged stumps. Few people had received any kind of first aid, and the ward hummed with moaning monotones, broken now and then by sudden shrieks of pain and cries of despair. Only the unconscious and dead were at peace.

Johnny! Oh, God! Johnny, forgive me!

The Emergency Room and surgery were immediately swamped, and it was some time before I found Dr. Mahoney on the cluttered ward. "Goddamn it! If some of these people don't get to surgery right away, it'll be too late!" he was saying.

"Doctor, do you know why we weren't called when they started coming in?"

"Who had time for that? Who in hell's running this show, anyway?"

Neither Captain Boyle nor the executive captain were visible. They had sought shelter in the old Spanish cistern, but once the all-clear sounded, the two captains consulted with the rear admiral. Yes, they should make immediate arrangements to relocate the hospital, transfer our casualties to Manila, and bury the dead. They hastily accepted the Philippine Union College in Balintawak, out in the countryside northeast of Manila. Then, after saving close to seven of the sixty tons of food in the Navy's bodega for the hospital, Captain Boyle turned the rest over to the Philippine Red Cross.

Meanwhile, on Ward C the coordinating task fell into Miss Redecker's lap, with only Chief Roberts to assist her.

The telephone and power lines were down, and power from the auxiliary unit was being directed to the surgery suites on the third floor and the Emergency Room. The elevators were inoperable.

"That isn't all, ma'am," a corpsman told me, "there isn't enough steam to operate the autoclave or bring the water in the instrument sterilizer to a boil. Doc Mahoney said to reuse the syringes if we have to, but change to sterile needles. Now we're running out of those." They were supposed to give one-quarter grain of morphine to all conscious patients.

I checked out the treatment room and discovered a dirty, dungaree-clad sailor working there. "What do you think you're doing here?" I snapped.

Pharmacist's Mate Berle answered, "Ma'am, he's helping me out."

Two other equally dirty soldiers were manning an unsightly gurney, not taking patients to surgery, but to the morgue, and then corpsmen would lift patients from the floor onto the beds without changing the linen. That can't be helped, I thought, but how many of them will die from infections, if not from their injuries?

"After all the goof-ups you fellows have made in the past, you're doing great now," I said, in an effort to applaud their teamwork.

"Yeah, we know," Cassidy said with a grin.

"I'm proud of you all, but how do you know who's who, who's had morphine and who hasn't?"

"Ma'am, I know who *I* gave shots to," and that was the way it stood.

Where to begin? First, the needles. See that the sailor keeps his hands clean. Show him the correct way to clean the needles and chemically sterilize them. Next, find a means of at least keeping a tentative record identifying the patients and showing when their shots were given.

"Sorry, ma'am, this is all I could find," said the sober-faced Bornowski from Medical Records as he gave me a box of mortuary tags.

I began talking to the wounded. "Be patient," I said. "We'll have a bed for you before long and get you cleaned up. Do you know when you had your shot? Would you like a sip of water?" As they responded, I copied their names, serial numbers, and blood types from their dog tags, and abbreviated whatever other information I learned.

"I'm attaching this tag to your wrist until we get charts made up. Hope it doesn't bother you."

For unconscious patients it was name, rank, or rating from their dog tags, and whatever I could observe about their condition.

"Have you had a shot, Fuller?" I asked, attaching a tag to his wrist.

"Yes, ma'am. Oh, God, nurse, you can't believe what it was like!"

"I'm beginning to get a pretty good idea," I said, and he seemed both grateful and embarrassed when I wiped the dirt and tears from his face. "Okay, now? I'll be back and check on you again."

Sitting on the floor was a tearful old Filipino woman and her equally distressed daughter, both in need of surgical attention. Not so her thumb-sucking grandchild, who sat wide-eyed as he took it all in. I knelt beside them and softly asked questions while I recorded their names.

"Marciano, he dead," the daughter managed to say, and the old woman cried along with her. Yes, it was Marciano our chef, and I added a few tears of my own when I told them how much he had meant to us in the Nurses Quarters.

Burned patients, shivering and glassy-eyed, would not have recognized themselves in a mirror. Some were barely breathing; others were sweaty as serum oozed from their burns. Emotionally disturbed patients hyperventilated, while others cried and cursed despairingly, ignoring their wounds. "Our shells just weren't reaching those sons of bitches!"

"My buddy was there one minute, and then he just wasn't!"

"Miss Still," a shaky voice said, "bet you didn't expect me back so soon."

"Hartman? Is that you under all that dirt? What happened? Did you zig when you should have zagged?"

"If I'd zagged, ma'am, I wouldn't be here," he

said weakly. "My leg got busted when the radio tower came down."

"I thought you would be on the *Langley*."

"Naw. No transportation. Being a radioman, they sent me over to the radio station."

"You feeling okay? You've had your shot?"

"My leg's numb," he said, and I turned back the sheet to find that his foot was becoming dangerously cyanotic.

"Cassidy, I released the tourniquet on Hartman's leg for a short while. It's still bleeding somewhat, and I put it back on, but not so tight. Will you keep an eye on it? Hartman, is the radio station getting any messages in or out?"

"Can't rightly say, but sure as day's day and night's night, Pearl Harbor got caught, if you'll excuse the expression ma'am, with its pants down."

"What about our fleet? Where is it?"

"Haven't heard. Must still be down south. Aw, hell, ma'am, I don't have time to be laid up like this!"

"Guess you'll have to take the time, won't you?" I joked, and went on to the next trembling patient.

"And nurse, I was standing down the road a piece when a bomb hit the dispensary and blew it to pieces." Atkins and Smith? Oh, NO. "And I had just carried my best friend over there, and —"

I sympathized with what he was saying as I put the tag on his wrist, but I was thinking about our corpsmen. My boys, my brothers, so like kinfolk. They have to be safe, they have to be. But, of course, they weren't.

It had been a wild afternoon, but now that the daylight was fading, the ward was pretty well organized. Civilian patients, sedated and wounds dressed, were sent home or to a makeshift hospital that was set up in Caridad. Patients going to and coming from surgery dwindled. Most of the dying were already dead. And now, the records.

Liz came over to help put the charts together, and in the dim auxiliary light, as I wandered up and down the aisles to check on patients, my mind was on other things.

It's just as well the rest of the fleet isn't here. Our aircraft don't have the same ferocious sound as the fighters and bombers going overhead. They can't help but do better out in the open sea. Oh, God, can you hear me? I'm not asking favors for myself. I don't deserve them, but please, oh, please watch over Johnny and the *Houston*!

"Nurse," a patient called softly.

"Having trouble going to sleep?" I whispered, automatically taking his wrist to check his name, pulse, and medications. "Would you like a tiny sip of water to moisten your mouth?"

"Naw."

"Are you uncomfortable?"

"You know what? I'm going to die."

"Oh, come on, Peterson. What a gloomy thing to say!"

In the dim light, he showed no evidence of distress. Sedated, but alert, eyes reasonably clear, skin pallid. Hardly the picture of a dying man. "After what you've been through, you can't help but be in shock," I said, wiping his face with a damp washcloth. "That's to be expected. I know how rough this must be, but your pulse is good. You're going to be just fine."

His pulse was actually, well, not that good. Thready but not unduly rapid, considering the circumstances.

"It's true, ma'am. I'm going to die."

"I guess we all will someday," I said chidingly, taking his hand in both of mine. "You mustn't talk like that. By tomorrow everything will look much brighter. Really it will."

"Not for me," he said with detached acceptance. "I heard the doc tell the surgery nurse that there was no use trying to sew me up 'cause I'd be dead before the night was out."

Oh, my! What a dreadful thing to say in front of a patient, even if it was probably true. He couldn't have said that.

"You must have misunderstood what was being said. You've been out of surgery quite a while. You're okay, and you mustn't worry yourself to pieces. Before you know it, you'll be up and on your feet again."

"The doc told 'em to put heavy dressings on me and send me out to the ward. See for yourself."

I didn't want to, but to satisfy him, I pulled

back the covers. Under a piece of rubberized sheeting, a doubled-up surgical warming blanket was heavy with blood and serum, and when I lifted it, I could hardly keep from gagging. Fecal matter oozed from his exposed intestines. Most of the surface flesh was gone, and there certainly wasn't enough skin left to make a closure. Oh, God in heaven, how can he still be alive? Short of a miracle, his chances for survival were absolutely zilch.

Many of our patients had already died. It was a matter of time before some who were still breathing would be dead, but not one of them was aware that he was dying. Except for Peterson.

What can I say? What can I do? I've seen many people die. Talking to the dying is never easy. It's hard enough for a doctor to tell family members that a patient is dying. Some of them don't have the stomach even to do that. Tell a patient he's dying? No! The accepted policy is to give hope where hope is nonexistent. This man knows he's dying, and he'll know I'm not being honest if I try to convince him otherwise.

Even so, all I could think of was, "You must have misunderstood." A wan smile crossed his face.

Holding his hand in both of mine, I weakly said, "Listen, Peterson, I'll be back shortly. You aren't having any pain, are you?"

I checked on other patients and made sure their records were ready to go with them to Manila. Records are important and I struggled to keep them straight, but mostly the struggle was within me, about my dying patient.

Oh heck, I thought, finally, the best way is a straightforward approach. I'll ask him if there's anything he would like me to do for him. It won't be easy, but what else can I do?

But when I went back to his bed, he wasn't there. "Yeah, the doc pronounced him dead maybe five or ten minutes ago."

Oh no, oh no! I could have asked him where he was from, could have asked about his next of kin, could have offered to take a message to his mother, wife, sweetheart . . . oh, how I failed him. I promised I'd be back, and he needed someone to talk to. He wanted my help and I didn't have the courage to give it until it was already too late.

"Ma'am?" Baldwin said, but I couldn't answer as I rushed outside, where I cried unabatedly.

At last, gaining my composure, I dried my eyes on my shirttail and returned to the ward's office. "Dottie," Liz said knowingly, "there's coffee and sandwiches in the kitchen."

"Sounds good," I said, grateful for the dim lights.

It was nearing 2200, and most of the patients had been transferred out. Dr. Mahoney, Baldwin, and Carmody were in the ward's kitchen hashing over some of the day's events when in staggered the two sailors who had been manning the mortuary gurney.

"Hey, ya got some ninety-proof booze handy?"

"Would some ninety-proof java do?"

81

"Kee-rist! Did we ever get the bejesus scared out of us!" one of them said as Liz pressed a steaming coffee cup into his trembling hands. " 'Scuse me, ma'am, that is, thank you, ma'am."

"What's the matter, Letterman?" Carmody asked. "Are the dead flying away?"

"Well, damn close to it!"

"Yeah," the other one said, "we're taking another body out. It's dark, ya know? We're tryin' to find a place to put this one, when one of the stiffs sits up 'n asks for a drink of water!"

7

ORDER AMID CHAOS

The busy two hospital captains still weren't here, and in trying to find a place for our patients in Manila, Miss Redecker contacted the fleet surgeon. He talked to Sternberg Hospital's commanding officer, who suggested using one of the nearby Estado Mayor's empty Army barracks as a temporary port in a storm. The 41st Infantry was out in the field, he said.

Transportation was needed, and for the next two hours, the fleet surgeon set out to corner every available means he could find, on wheels or afloat. It was a slow and tedious process, but around 2200, Miss Redecker and Liz were among the hospital staff who went out with the first patients. Things speeded up considerably when the PT boats came to the rescue.

It was not until after midnight that transportation was ready for the remaining patients on wards B and C, and with our suitcases in hand, Joyce and I trudged doggedly over to the dock with the corpsmen and ambulatory patients.

"It ain't what it used to be," Joyce commented dully.

"No, it sure isn't."

My fantasyland was lifeless and stripped of familiar landmarks. Only reflections of sporadic flames flaring up in the Navy Yard danced across the water. No cheerful breeze, no chirping geckos, no singing crickets, no music from rattling palm fronds. Just a cold and ugly night. Never again would I see the glowing amber lights in the little lighthouses; never again would I sit alone by the farthest one to solve my problems. But I had not a single tear to shed.

"Is this our transportation?" Joyce mumbled, looking at the PT boat moored next to the dock. "Geez, it looks like an oversize speedboat. What's it doing with torpedoes?"

"You got me. Maybe it delivers them to submarines. Oh," I said to the boat's captain, who was leaning against one of the torpedoes.

"Looks like it's too long to be a speedboat," Joyce said, "but is it?"

"You could say so. It's seventy feet long, to be exact," he said, as patients began boarding.

"Do you deliver these torpedoes to the submarines?"

"Whenever we can," he said with a chuckle, "depending on whose subs they are, of course."

"How fast does it go?" Joyce asked tiredly.

"Pretty fast. It has three 1,250-horsepower Packard engines. Her top speed is around 45 knots, and when we launch one of these fish —"

"You shoot torpedoes from *this?*"

84

"We sure as hell do," was the only explanation he offered.

When all the patients were aboard, I was going to join them in the crew's quarters below. But it was so stifling down there that I asked Ensign Grant if we could ride up front, out in the open air.

"Sure, but it gets pretty cold." Joyce decided not to join me.

With a powerful roar of the engines, the pilot deftly spun the craft toward Manila, but then Grant and the pilot decided to take her over closer to the Navy Yard. Since this was their last run from the hospital, I figured there was something they wanted to check out or take a last look at. Whatever the reason, with its engines purring quietly, the boat glided ever so slowly.

What was left of the Yard was a ghastly sight. The silhouette I knew so well — towers, tanks, cranes, structures — was transformed into a diabolical graveyard. Distorted objects jutted up heinously among scattered and smoldering ruins. A solitary smokestack stood like a sentinel watching over its freakish charges. A lone pier looked as though a gigantic monster had picked it up, twisted it out of shape, and thrown it back. An occasional flame burst out in bizarre dance-of-death configurations against the night sky, and the awesome quiet that settled over the island made it seem disrespectful to speak above a whisper.

Oh my God, how could this have happened? I

thought as the pilot kept the boat at a safe distance from the large chunks of debris floating in the water.

"Ensign Grant," I whispered, "I heard the *Sealion* got a direct hit."

"Yeah," he answered. "Its bow is sticking up right next to the wharf where it was tied."

"What about the *Seadragon*? It was tied next to the *Sealion*."

"It's not there now."

"Was it sunk?" I whispered, not really wanting to know the horrible truth, and Grant didn't hear me anyway. I remembered the laughing faces of the submarine officers when I'd seen them last. Now they were all entombed in their distorted and misshapen ships.

Johnny, are you dead too? Is your ship on the bottom of the ocean? Oh no. No, that can't be.

I shivered, not only from the chilly salt air, but from thoughts of friends already lost to the war, and from the horrendous damage done to the Navy base. Its enormity was beyond belief, too macabre and gruesome for words, and I stared at it all as if in a hypnotic state.

"There's what's left of our warehouses," Grant said, saddened by the loss of precious spare parts so urgently needed to maintain their boats, and after he and the pilot talked a little longer, they had had enough. We all watched closely while the pilot cleared a path through the ships, tugboats, and barges that tilted crazily in the water.

"Okay, let's go," he said, and with its Packard

engines roaring, the boat split the calm surface of the water, a spray of flourescent water flying out and away from its bow. In what seemed no more than seconds, the pilot brought it neatly up to the Lagaspi Landing.

"For a boat as heavy as this," I heard the corpsman say, "it sure flies through the air."

"To tell you the truth, it's not as heavy as it looks. Under that gray paint is a plywood hull. It has no metal armor at all."

Noonday raids made one's hair stand on end, especially when Standard Oil's barges were coming down to the Pasig River from their Pandacan District refineries. The Estado Mayor compound bordered the river, and the high-pitched whistle of released bombs followed by their deafening roar made the wooden barracks seem like a tremendous bonfire about to happen.

"Nurse, next time you'd better hit the deck," a patient said, and I probably would have, if I had not been so petrified. "If you can hear it whistling, it'll hit beyond you and . . ."

The Estado Mayor barracks didn't make much of a hospital, so Captain Boyle accepted the Philippine Union College in Balintawak as an alternative. Tasks such as wiring a room for surgery, adding more toilet and shower facilities, screening the windows, and sinking a 350-foot well were bothersome, but it was out in the countryside and far enough north of Manila that its function as a hospital was of no interest to the Japanese military.

In the meantime, the combined Army and Navy medical corps set up surgical teams in the city so that emergency care could be given on the spot to servicemen and civilians. Each team was to accept all casualties that came through their doors. As soon as their conditions warranted it, civilians were sent to one of the city's hospitals, soldiers to Sternberg, sailors to Balintawak. Ellen and Joyce were assigned to the Holy Ghost College; Harriet to Santa Scholastica College as a part of a Navy operating-room team; and Sarah, Velda, and I to the Jai Alai Building. The others were to remain with the medical unit at Balintawak.

Both Sarah and Velda had already sent telegrams home, and this was my last chance to do the same. When I saw the line at the Western Union office in the Manila Hotel I knew it would take forever, but it was now or never, so I stayed.

How surprised Johnny would be to see this, I thought. It used to be a dignified gardenlike setting with background music, fragrant with ginger flowers and ilang-ilang blossoms, a lobby where military top brass mingled with tuxedoed civilians, stylish ladies, and important Filipinos. Now it was a constant hum of anxious voices, wrinkled uniforms, crumpled hats, sweaty bodies, and stale cigarette and cigar smoke.

"Hey fellas! Look who's here! Dottie! Am I ever glad to see you!" one of the *Sealion* officers said, and except for the captain, the ship's entire group of officers stopped to talk to me.

"We've been worried about you nurses. Is everyone okay?"

"Yes, but I can't believe this! Is it really you?" I touched each of them to make sure. "I thought you all had gone down with your ship!"

"We were in the Army Navy Club during the raid, and we found out a bomb exploded in our engine room and did the *Sealion* in. We've lost some fine men. Some damned fine men. We're going to miss them."

"So now the Grand Old Lady, the *Canopus*, is our home while the skipper works out something with Admiral Hart. You must've seen the *Canopus* in the bay. She's a converted passenger liner made into a mini Navy Yard."

"That white ship that was anchored near Sangley Point not long ago?"

"It's not white now: they've splashed different shades of paint all over her to make her blend into the shoreline on the other side of the Pasig River, and darned if it doesn't look like a part of the scenery!"

I listened happily to their lively chatter, but I wondered how they could be so high-spirited when their friends on the *Seadragon* had been lost. I eventually had a chance to tell them about the ride on the PT boat and about Ensign Grant's having seen the *Sealion*'s bow sticking up out of the water, and how bad I'd felt knowing the *Seadragon* was sunk there beside it.

"Honey, the *Seadragon* didn't go down."

"It didn't?"

"Only one man got hurt. A corpsman, I think, coming out of the conning tower, but that was all." Collectively they praised the skipper of the submarine rescue ship, the *Pigeon*, which had nosed its bow between the two submarines and shoved the *Seadragon* away from the burning *Sealion*.

"He deserves a medal. The *Pigeon* carries a helluva load of fuel. Thank God it wasn't hit!"

"And, my dear girl, Ensign Grant couldn't have seen the *Seadragon*, because the *Pigeon* towed it out far enough so that it could submerge."

"Dottie, we'd love to visit longer but we're running out of time." With good-bye hugs, kisses, and good-luck wishes, they left.

I sighed with relief, knowing they all were safe. It just goes to show how foolish it is to jump to conclusions, I thought, and by golly, until I positively know otherwise, Johnny is alive and well.

Meanwhile, waiting in line so long made me more and more nervous by the minute. I knew I should be over at the Jai Alai Building helping to set it up as a hospital.

Well, for goodness' sake, I thought, that looks like Jamie, but she's wearing a khaki Army officer's field uniform. Velda and I had met her on our vacation at the Army's Camp John Hay recreation center, when she'd been wearing ordinary sports clothes. The only other Army nurses we'd seen wore white uniforms on duty.

"Jamie?" I called out tentatively as she passed by, and it was her. "In your officer's uniform, I wasn't even sure it was you," I said. "When did the Army Nurse Corps commission its nurses?"

She was surprised to learn that Navy nurses didn't have officer status, and although she was a little fuzzy about the facts, she said it had something to do with the 1920 Army Reorganization Act. Granting Army nurses a commission had apparently been a result of their praiseworthy accomplishments while on active duty in Europe. They'd been granted a relative officer status ranging from second lieutenant to major, with authority directly under the medical officers. In practice this was the same as our noncommissioned Navy nurses, and our pay levels, based on longevity, were equal.

We chatted for a few more minutes, and she told me about the tremendous influx of Army Reserve nurses who had recently been sent to the Philippines.

Time passed slowly. Oh, heck, I thought, now they're drawing the blackout curtains. I swear, these people must be sending telegrams to each of their relatives individually, and to everyone else they know.

"You never know who you're going to run into," a voice whispered suddenly into my ear.

"Maury! Oh my goodness, look at you! So it's Major Randall, no less!"

"Sure is," he said proudly. "Now you stay right here. Don't go away." He left to go get two San

Miguel beers and a dish of peanuts from the bar.

No, he hadn't heard anything about Sam and his regiment. All the Marines had been ordered out of China, and two commercial passenger liners, the *President Harrison* and the *President Madison*, had been used as transport ships. Most of the Marines had been in Shanghai, and both ships had been needed to bring them and the American civilians out. The *Harrison* had since gone back to pick up the Marines and the embassy staff in Tsingtao, but Maury didn't know if it had returned. (We would later discover that Japanese destroyers escorted the unarmed ship into the South China Sea. When Pearl Harbor was bombed they forced it to stop, and Sam became one of Japan's first American prisoners of war.)

Maury, God love him, could see how anxious I was, and to get my mind on something else, he soon had me and everyone close by laughing. He told us about the unofficial passenger who'd been tucked away among their personal effects, a four-legged private first class named Soochow. As a newborn pup, he'd been picked up by one of the enlisted Marines in the reeds along the Soochow River, where Chinese boat people feasted on dog stew. He'd gradually become part of the Corps, assuming duty with the Marines at the gate and barking at anyone not wearing a Marine uniform. He'd marched with the Marines on parade and attached himself to Company B at night. They'd begun to think the independent mutt considered himself an officer. He'd worked his way up to corporal before being busted for peeing on the flagpole.

Before I knew it I was at the head of the line. Maury had been a godsend and, as with the *Sealion* submariners, it was a hug, a kiss, and good-luck wishes. The telegrapher laughed when I asked him if it was still 12 December as I handed him my message.

CHRISTMAS GREETINGS — AM OKAY IN MANILA — DON'T WORRY ABOUT ME — LOVE DOROTHY

By now it was pitch black outside. With heavily shaded headlights, taxicabs that crept in under the hotel's portico were met by an avalanche of people. I couldn't wait for that, and trusting I'd be able to find my way, I bravely set off on foot. Just as I reached the street, a sedan was pulling into the hotel's circular drive. I walked alongside it and said to the driver, "I'm on a military surgical team being set up in the Jai Alai Building. Please, it's urgent. Can you take me there?"

"Sorry ma'am," he said, but then the limousine stopped a few feet ahead, and its passenger got out.

"Having a problem?"

"You might say so," I told the darkened figure. "I'm assigned to one of the Army and Navy surgical teams, and —"

"An Army nurse?"

"No sir. A Navy nurse."

After telling his chauffeur to take me to my destination, he vanished into the night so quickly that I didn't have a chance to thank him.

Savoring the comfort of the dusty sedan, I said, "Driver, please thank that fine gentleman if you ever see him again."

"I'll do that ma'am." Then he added proudly, "That is General Douglas MacArthur."

8

ON THE MOVE

This once-beautiful Jai Alai Building with its wide-open spaces had always been awe-inspiring to me. In the Skyroom on the fourth level, Johnny and I had dined by candlelight and watched the graceful motions of the players on the court below, so dashing in their colorful costumes. We had danced to Sammy Lahr's band, but all that was just a memory now. The building's owners had removed its plush red carpets, drapes, and furnishings, and the second- and third-level balconies looked as forsaken as the Skyroom. On my arrival I was welcomed by the thunder of metal beds being set up on the court. The sound bounced from wall to wall, from floor to ceiling and back again.

In the daylight hours we could see the walled city beyond the legislative building and other familiar structures, but right now our team had little time for viewing anything. The building's insulation muffled the outside traffic noise if not the terrifying roar of bombers and fighters, which sent shock waves echoing throughout its cavernous interiors.

"Geez, it's enough to scare the patients to death," a corpsman said.

"It scares the hell out of me," added another one, "but hell, man, if your name's on a tomb, that's the way it is."

Such logic is reasonable enough, I thought, but we had little time to worry about it or anything else. By the end of the following day, with three doctors, three nurses, and thirty or so Army and Navy corpsmen, we were ready to take on almost anything that came in.

The next day went by, then the next, and despite the huge sign out front in both English and Tagalog, no patients showed up after the daily noon raids. Zero fighters seemed so close that our spooked team began to wonder if our first patients would not be Japanese.

"There must be thousands of casualties out there. Why aren't they being brought in?"

"Enjoy the rest while you can, Dorothy," Sarah said and turned to the next page in her magazine.

"Give them time," the Army's Dr. Schultz added, as he placed a red queen of hearts on a black king of clubs.

Portable radios were on constantly. Reports from San Francisco covered mainly what was going on in Finland and Austria, and how encouraged the British were, knowing that American troops would be joining them. From a Japanese radio station, Tokyo Rose murmured in a sexy, syrupy voice, "Oooh, hello there, fellas. Had enough of the Emperor's Eagles?" And from the Army's Victory Broadcast on Corregidor, "Reinforcement to MacArthur's USAFFE will give General Homma plenty to worry about."

Suspense intensified with prolonged inactivity, and tempers flared. Everyone was edgy. I couldn't stand Velda with her pouting and scowling, and I guess my impatience made the feelings mutual. Air raids came and went, like our apathetic games of rummy, poker, bridge, and solitaire.

"Looks like they're hitting the walled city again," someone said.

"Bombing heavier today than yesterday."

"Wow! That one was close."

Newspapers offered no relief, except for the comics. 23 December came and still no patients.

"They must be admitting them somewhere. Holy Ghost? Santa Scholastica? Balintawak? Why not here?"

"Hadn't we better call Miss Redecker?"

"I did," Sarah said, not seeming to miss a word in the book she was reading.

"I'm going up to the top deck, that's if it's okay with you," I said hatefully.

Fortunately no one else was up there. Christmas decorations on the streets below were noticeable by their absence. Just lots of military traffic. As terrifying as it was when the Yard was bombed, I thought, at least we were doing something useful!

No, no! No tears! Think about something positive. Home. Poor Mom and Dad, how worried they must be. Think of something else.

I wandered around the empty dining room, trying unsuccessfully to see its tables with their impeccable linen, flickering candles, polished silverware, and delicious food served by the smartly uniformed waiters. I walked over to where the balcony's outside tables had been, and looking down at the jai alai court, I tried to envision the players as they sent the ball ricocheting from one wall to the other. That didn't work either. The rows of neatly made beds wouldn't go away.

If this goes on much longer, I'll go out of my mind!

I wandered out on the dance floor. Halfway across, I began to hum and waltz, imagining Johnny's arms around me, his laughing eyes looking into mine.

If you were the only girl in the world,
And I were the only boy . . .

Maybe I'd misjudged him. He'd been so drunk, he probably hadn't understood what Jake had said. Again the tears welled up, and this time I couldn't control them. Is the *Houston* lying on the bottom of the ocean? Is he dead? Oh no, oh no, don't jump to conclusions! Dear God, if only I knew how to pray!

I heard the echo of the elevator doors and rushed out of sight. I brushed away the tears, took a deep breath, lit a cigarette, and looked out the window.

"Miss Still? Dorothy? Are you up here?"

"Paul? Oh, thank goodness! You came to tell us we're finally going to get out of here!"

"I came to bring Christmas presents for you nurses," he said, hat perched at its usual jaunty angle, and he clowningly apologized for its crumpled appearance.

"How nice, and thank you," but I already knew what was in it. Miss Redecker and Julia had designed coat-styled uniforms, and Josie had arranged to have two of them made for each of us. Now, with our Nurse Corps pins on the collars, we could at least look official. I showed one of them to Paul and asked if he thought the superintendent of the Nurse Corps would approve. He said he'd fire her if she didn't.

"I'm so glad to see you. Tell me what it's like at Balintawak. Are you getting many patients?"

"One or two. Guess most of our Navy men have joined the Army. Not many around here anymore."

"Well, tell me, what are the other teams doing?"

"Holy Ghost gets more locals than servicemen. From what I hear, Santa Scholastica has a bigger setup, and they're doing a thriving business. That's about all I can tell you."

I went down on the elevator with him, and before he could leave, the rest of the team plied him with questions. As for war news, he had little to offer that we hadn't already heard on the radio, but his presence and funny tales boosted our morale considerably.

"Paul, would you mind taking me over to Aguinaldo's Department Store before you go back?"

"Shouldn't, but I will."

The slow-moving traffic was worse than it seemed from the top-floor windows, and I said, "Oh, I'm so glad to get out of there. Thank you."

"That's the only reason you're here. And you're welcome. I think."

"Why do you suppose the merchants are boarding up their windows?"

He had no answer for that, but he knew why the traffic was so bad.

"MacArthur declared Manila an open city," he said.

"What does that mean?"

"Our military's moving out. Soldiers are coming in from all over the island, heading for Bataan. One guy told me his unit had spent days coming up from Lucerna."

"What's Captain Boyle doing about this?"

"Don't think he knows, but I'd better get back and find out."

With this news, Jai Alai's lassitude changed. At last we would be doing something worthwhile, and soon. Velda became her bubbly self again and our whole team worked well into the night. By then only a few beds remained standing, just in case. The others were dismantled, bed frames folded, mattresses stacked, and bed linen packed.

Nearly everything else was boxed. Personal effects were stuffed back into suitcases and duffle bags, and we were ready to move.

Nothing developed on the next day. From the top-floor windows, the crowded traffic could be heard as it lumbered along as quickly as possible. Demolition crews began blowing up fuel tanks and other immovable military equipment, and we could see some of the civilians scurrying around on the streets.

On Christmas Eve, Dr. Schultz said, "Anyone interested in going to midnight mass?" Convinced that this was indeed a time for prayer, Velda and I joined him and the Catholic corpsmen.

It was scary in the dark on the way to the cathedral. Shouting Filipinos were looting everything they could move. "Merry Christmas!" they called out in Tagalog, offering bottles of champagne to the doctor and the corpsmen, but we all hurried on.

I had never been in a Catholic church before, and I enjoyed the colorful Christmas decorations in the candlelight. The congregation seemed to show sincere trust in their faith, and everything seemed full of mystery, with the Latin and a Tagalog sermon. The choir's childlike voices were as eloquent as the extraordinary tones that came from the pipe organ's bamboo reeds, but most impressive of all was the peaceful tranquillity within these ancient walls that seemed to lock out the troubled world.

If you can hear me, God, please get us out of the city before it's too late, but obviously God wasn't listening to the likes of me.

On Christmas morning Dr. Schultz and the Army corpsmen hitched a ride out to Bataan. Had not Paul said he would be back to get us, we would have been tempted to join them.

"Oooh, what a shame," said Tokyo Rose from the crackly radio. "You boys are going to miss Santa Claus this year. Too bad. Is your sweetie enjoying someone else's kisses? Does your mama miss you? Can't you taste her delicious Christmas dinner? Her apple pies?"

"General MacArthur again assures us that help is . . ."

"City officials ask that residents remain calm and . . ."

"Looters will be . . ."

Raising a glass of warm champagne, Dr. Shackleford said, "Merry Christmas." Dr. Kleinfeldt added, "Bah, humbug!"

Word that MacArthur had declared Manila an open city came to Admiral Hart from the general's headquarters so late that he had almost no time to order the *Canopus* to proceed to Mariveles Harbor and to move into the Marines' tunnels on Corregidor's Monkey Point. Here he must have concluded that he had best join his fleet, and off to Java he went with not even so much as a "Hostilities have begun; act accordingly" message for the Medical Corps.

26 December started as dully as Christmas day, and our disheartened team ate lunch listlessly. Another hour passed before Paul yelled, "Is everybody ready?"

"You said it!"

"Where are we going?"

"Santa Scholastica! Come on! Come on!" And, while the Army's tanks, trucks, and weapon carriers headed toward Bataan, Paul drove our station wagon in the opposite direction.

VROOM! VROOM! went demolition explosions along the waterfront, one after another.

Farther down Taft Avenue, we could vaguely see what was left of the Navy Yard. There were voluminous black clouds when the remaining oil tanks on Sangley Point were torched, and moments later the Yard itself turned into a massive fireball. The station wagon shuddered from shock waves as the ammunition dump blew sky-high.

When we came to the back gate of the campus, Army trucks were hauling personnel and supplies out as our Navy trucks were hauling them in.

"Aren't we going to take that stuff with us?"

"We're not going anywhere."

9

MANILA OCCUPIED

Owned and operated by nuns in the Catholic German convent, Santa Scholastica College was in the elite Malate district. In keeping with its neighborhood, the two-storied building was Spanish in design with a decorative wrought-iron fence across the front and high stone walls that enclosed its twenty-acre campus.

This musical college for young women was an excellent choice for the Army's intended purposes. An auditorium with its balcony was ideal for a storeroom, and two sizable dormitories housed their personnel. There were kitchen and dining facilities, and numerous classrooms that converted nicely into wards. Farther out were the utility rooms and a parking area. The only out-of-bounds was beyond the locked doors that opened into the sisters' cloister.

The Army made such a fast exodus that their heavier equipment, supplies, and patients were left behind — but not the Navy's operating-room team, which included Harriet, a Navy surgeon, and four of our corpsmen. Grabbing her packed bag, Harriet mumbled something about not

104

wanting to be here when the Japanese came in and, along with the rest of the surgical team, she was gone.

Olga solemnly stared off into space. Liz thought that Harriet was AWOL and should be court-martialed after the war. Ellen was tearful; Amy retreated to her dormitory room; Joyce lit a cigarette; Velda reverted to pouting and self-abasement; Bobbie gloomily meandered over to the galley.

The Big Three had little to say, and this was the last straw for me.

On Sunday 28 December, Joyce said, "Dottie, Olga and I are going downtown to the eleven o'clock mass. Want to go with us?"

Manila was like a ghost town. A third of its citizens had fled to Bataan along with the Army but, as might be expected, the Santa María Church was packed with worried and concerned citizens. This mass lacked the radiance and tranquillity of the midnight mass in the cathedral, not that the Catholics were any less sincere. As for me, to pray and ask favors from someone or something as fanciful as a God in heaven was sure to be an unproductive exercise, but why not?

God, please don't let me be so nervous, and forget what I wrote. Please keep Johnny and the *Houston* safe. The whole Asiatic fleet for that matter. Take care of Harriet, our sailors and soldiers, our Marines, Maury and Sam, wherever they are, and everyone else I should pray for. Thanks, God, if You are listening.

105

After mass we stopped at the Bay View Hotel for lunch. It was crowded with passengers who had come ashore from cruise ships that were anchored in Manila Bay on that fateful day. Following Admiral Hart's advice, captains of these ships were headed for Australia post haste. As a result, some of these people had only a few traveler's checks. Some came ashore planning to stay a few days, others had only an overnight bag, and still others had no more than the clothes they were wearing.

"Geez, what a dilemma," Joyce said, and we thanked our lucky stars. All of our possessions were in the auditorium at Santa Scholastica.

After lunch, I picked up a copy of the *Manila Tribune*, where I read things like "the United States Navy is following an intensive and well-planned campaign against Japanese forces which will result in positive assistance in the defense of the Philippine Islands."

I also read that representatives from the High Commissioner's office and the Malacañang Palace had been contacted by the Japanese Army of Occupation: "Incoming forces will be small, and the transition to our authority will be orderly and quiet."

By the time all of the eighty-four Army patients plus servicemen found in the city hospitals were added to our roster, the ratio of patients to staff was three to one. On 31 December, we were really jolted when the Army patients were rushed down to the port area to be taken aboard an inner-island ship bearing a huge red cross. Why not our Navy patients? In any case, this brought the ratio close to a one-to-one basis.

Drs. Shackleford and Edwards had advised everyone not to unpack. "We'll be evacuated any minute now," they had said. But by New Year's Eve all hope was gone. Standing on the roof, we toasted one another with Scotch without rocks as we watched the city's lights sparkle once again.

On New Year's Day the local radio station went off the air. Free copies of the *Manila Tribune*'s final edition reiterated statements regarding the forthcoming Japanese entry into the city. Civilians should carry on normal peacetime pursuits, be respectful, obey the occupying forces. Captain Boyle ordered the hospital personnel to wear the usual white or khaki uniforms while on duty.

On 2 January a bicycle brigade, marching soldiers, trucks, and official cars came into the city. We could hear the Japanese civilians interned in the Rizal stadium shouting "Bonzai! Bonzai!" but except for guards camped across the street, Santa Scholastica was ignored.

As of this date, Bornowski accounted for all present in the daily log, naming three captains (Captain Boyle, the executive officer, and the fleet surgeon), twelve doctors, five dentists, two chaplains, four pharmacists, eleven nurses, thirteen cooks and mess attendants, one hundred five corpsmen, one hundred sixty patients, a Filipino nurse, and a stranded Catholic priest.

Commander Brennen, critically injured in the Navy Yard bombing, asked Miss Redecker to accept his Filipino wife as a Navy nurse as far as the Japanese were concerned, and she found no problem with this. Felicia had remained at her husband's bedside day and night from the beginning.

"Well, this brings our complement back up to the original twelve," Lizzy said, and I couldn't help but laugh. "Dottie, if Harriet and I had to live in tight quarters like this for long, we'd probably kill each other!"

On 3 January, not knowing what to expect, most of us remained outwardly and naively calm, but I was disgusted with some of the doctors who, I thought, should be setting an example of courage for the rest of us. One in particular was in a panic state, but not Commander Stewart or other doctors including Kleinfeldt, Mahoney, and Baker, who stoicly accepted what they could not change. Captain Boyle quoted the Geneva Convention regarding prisoners of war. According to him, our entire noncombatant staff and patients would be taken safely behind our own front lines.

The first Japanese proclamation came through the recently taken over *Manila Tribune*. For every violation of their orders, it said, there would be a ten-to-one reprisal. That sounded a bit ominous.

Finally, three Japanese officers came in with an interpreter, informed Captain Boyle that he and his command were prisoners of war, checked the contents of the safe, and left.

With this development, all guns and boxes of ammunition were deposited in one of the metal trash cans sitting against the back wall. When a joy-riding Japanese soldier drove a Chrysler sedan through the wall, he scared the daylights out of us, but thank goodness, he jumped out and disappeared in a hurry. A day or so later we ran for cover at the sound of gunshots within the campus, but it turned out to be the ammunition. Tightly sealed in the trash can, it had begun to explode from the heat.

Next, guards came in to relieve our MPs, but those assigned to the Master-at-Arms' desk and the OD were allowed to remain on duty. A series of inspections followed, first for radios, knives, firearms, and flashlights. With smiling faces, the guards pocketed whatever personal effects took their fancy. Seldom did the same guards stay longer than a few days, but each time different guards took over, there were more inspections and more looting.

Liz put her engagement ring in her cold cream jar, and her answer to why she hadn't married the guy was "Dumb me! I wanted to see the Philippines."

Women's personal effects, except for knives and flashlights, had little interest for the guards. They didn't bother our dormitory rooms, and there were few threatening moments during January. The Japanese officers were polite, in their own way. As time went by, conditions deteriorated. No means were taken to feed us. Captain Boyle had already cut meals to twice a day before the end of 1941, and guards going through the pantry had taken the canned pineapple and similar tasty items.

Captain Boyle protested loudly when the Japanese took the hospital's vehicles parked on the campus. It didn't help either when a visiting Japanese official thought the prisoners were too comfortable. Japanese soldiers installed a barbed-wire fence that cut off all of the campus from the main buildings. This left only the domestic washing machine from our Cañacao Nurses Quarters to handle the hospital's laundry.

Occasionally copies of the *Manila Tribune* came in. The sisters and the priests were a far better source of information, but this ended when the Japanese completely blocked off the cloister's locked doors. Then they confiscated our quinine, a vital drug in a country infested with malaria-carrying mosquitoes. Unused beds, mattresses, patients' hospital garments, and mosquito nets went out the gate, not to mention nets taken by individual guards.

Japanese doctors Tanaka and Anusa communicated through an interpreter, but more often than not it was sergeants down to privates who were left in charge. What a humiliating situation for our Navy officers, especially the three captains. Faces were slapped for silly reasons. The sergeant who went over the daily log with Bornowski would yell and jump to his feet repeatedly.

Bornowski would jump to attention, the sergeant would soundly slap his face, and then it was back to the log.

The guard outside went into a frenzy when bombs exploded somewhere toward Nichols Field. Then our gentle Dr. Baker got his face slapped when he suggested the panicky guards come inside. "Japanese don't need help from Americans!"

When two Filipino mess attendants were unaccounted for during the tenko (roll call) at 2100 hours, wild-eyed guards ran about menacingly, their bayoneted rifles drawn. The sergeant threatened grave consequences if there was another escape.

Then there was another one, while Liz was on duty. "Dear God, the sergeant was furious! 'Shoot patients on each side of his bed!' Then he said, 'Shoot nurses, too!' Oh, Blessed Mother of God, I knew I was going to die, and I hadn't made my last confession!"

No one was shot, but no one laughed either. Thereafter, tenko was held twice a day or whenever the bored guards chose to do so.

"Hell, who wants to learn to count in Japanese? Ichi, ni, san, shi!"

"If these dolts could count straight, we wouldn't have to stand here so long."

Inspections, more inspections. More supplies went out.

"Mr. Phillips was smart when he raffled off the

111

Ships Service Inventory before the Nips got here," Bobbie observed.

"What do I want with cigarettes?" Amy asked.

"Give them to these nicotine addicts," Lizzy suggested.

"Save them," Sarah said. "One of these days they'll be as good as gold." Somehow her advice had a ring of truth.

We worried when Hartman and the other radiomen were taken out for interrogations, and we sighed with relief when they were returned unharmed. As January ended, our patient-care routine continued halfheartedly. Our critical patients had either died or were well on the road to recovery.

Everyone knew that Captain Boyle and the fleet surgeon didn't hit it off. The other doctors mechanically made their prescribed rounds, and that didn't take much of their time. The dentists busied themselves cleaning everyone's teeth and filling cavities. One doctor had been scared stiff to begin with and now seemed to be heading for a complete nervous breakdown as the boring hours dragged by. The doctors had their enlisted "doggie-robbers," who washed their clothes and cared for their personal needs while they lost themselves in magazines, books, and jigsaw puzzles.

We nurses tended to our own needs. We were on the wards from 0700 to the 2100 curfew with no night duty. Oh, no, we weren't to tempt fate, even in semisecluded areas.

The corpsmen handled the hospital's endless

chores. They outnumbered the rest of us and could be selective in choosing their friends. They voluntarily held a kangaroo court when anyone got out of line, thus solving most of their own problems. With Jeffery Morse's cheerful disposition, what better place for them and the ambulating patients to shoot the breeze than around his bed.

As the days dragged by, Paul Phillips was a godsend for me. He taught me how to play cribbage, and we spent hours in the courtyard.

"Yesterday I was out hanging clothes on the line," I told him one day, pegging two points, "and a guard came over and said, 'Ohio.' I asked if he had been in Ohio, but whatever he said after that, I wouldn't know."

"It means 'hello.' "

"Is that so? Uh, oh. Speak of the devil."

Two guards came up, chattering something. With a little pantomiming, Paul said, "Cribbage."

"Cree-beege? Ah," and they happily said some more things, apparently pleased at having learned a new word. Paul offered them each a Chesterfield cigarette.

They bowed politely with more incomprehensible words, and then they offered Paul a Japanese cigarette. After a few more polite exchanges, they relieved Paul of his package of cigarettes.

Another day, a young Japanese officer sadly told us, "War is terrible, but it will end in a week or two, and we will send you home."

Ho, ho, ho, I thought. Who will be sending who home?

Amusing incidents helped. The two EENT doctors organized a spelling bee, but that fell flat. A songfest brought suspicious guards running in with their bayoneted rifles. Evening discussions in the courtyard helped lessen the boredom.

Lizzy and the young Irish priest, Father Reilly, would sometimes banter laughingly back and forth, and Bobbie said, "You're flirting with him, Liz, and you shouldn't do that. He's getting a crush on you."

"Don't be silly! For Gawd's sake, he's a priest!"

"He's a man first, a priest second, and don't forget that."

Father Reilly was a likable fellow who said mass every morning, and whether wishy-washy Catholics actually became more devout or were coerced by the fast-talking priest, attend they did. Trouble came when the Navy's Protestant chaplains took exception to the priest's soul-saving efforts. They claimed the Catholics were implying that only through the Catholic faith could one gain eternal peace.

On one of my darker days I asked Father Reilly if I might borrow a prayer book, and from then on, I was inundated with catechism and religious books that read more like fiction than fact.

"Let me baptize you," he said repeatedly, but no. This wasn't for me, and I dodged him whenever he came in my direction.

Later Father Reilly became acutely ill, so much

so that death seemed imminent. This was brought to Tanaka's attention, and apparently the Japanese had a deep respect for the dead in instances like this, because he allowed a priest to come in and give Father Reilly the Catholic last rites before he died. It saddened everyone to some extent, especially our Catholic nurses. It certainly saddened me. I shouldn't have been so rude to him, I thought.

As one day followed another, it was depressing to see Japanese aircraft heading toward Bataan, unnerving to hear the rumbling sounds from that direction and to see the flashes of light in the night sky.

Our situation deteriorated further when a group of patients, doctors, and corpsmen were sent to a "well-equipped hospital," and with them went more of our scarce medical supplies. Then even more patients, personnel, and supplies were sent to the new hospital. When a patient was sent back for an x-ray examination, he told us that Pasay was an elementary school, not a hospital. No beds, nothing except kid-size desks, and those were being used for firewood to cook the rice.

So where were all the supplies going?

Boredom intensified. Every book, magazine, and jigsaw puzzle made the circuit a second and third time. It was harder each day to maintain a cheerful attitude. Real or imaginary slights could sour one's disposition. Someone told the captain that someone else had picked a mango from the trees growing within our limited boundaries, and a notice appeared soon thereafter on the bulletin board:

13 February 1942
From: Commanding Officer
To: All Navy personnel

1. Fruit trees are to be considered out of bounds for unauthorized personnel.
2. Anyone violating this directive will be confined to his quarters for an unspecified time, being denied his rations for one day.

K. L. Boyle, Capt. MC, USN

Was this consistent with the pettiness involved, or was the captain being ironically humorous? Only he knew, but mangoes ripening on his window sill gave one reason to wonder.

Generally speaking, the nosy patients and corpsmen were putting on a good front and making the best of a bad situation. More often than not their inane chatter was meant to tease, but when it comes to gossip, women take a back seat. Ordinarily I tuned out such drivel, but one time when I was on the night shift and had an upset stomach and a splitting headache, talk about Velda came through loud and clear.

"For goodness' sake! If you can't say something nice about someone, shut up," I finally protested.

"But, ma'am —"

"If you don't stop it I'm going to put you, and you, and you, on report! Is that clear?"

When I got off duty I went right to bed, and by 0400 I was really sick. Hot one minute, shivering the next, and when I rushed to the bathroom to vomit, I found myself looking at the world through jaundiced eyes.

"All we need now is infectious hepatitis," Miss Redecker said irritably.

"I'm sorry."

"You are not as sorry as I am!"

I could hardly keep from shouting, "I didn't get sick on purpose!"

Had I known, she really wasn't as unfeeling as she sounded. She had reason enough to be filled with resentment. To her way of thinking, Captain Boyle had had no right to take a position on the nurses' behalf without consulting her first. Apparently he had suggested that only half of the nurses be sent to Santo Tomas. Then he had apparently asked Lieutenant Tanaka's approval for everyone else to go, as long as she stayed here! She saw no point in upsetting the nurses by telling them that Lieutenant Tanaka was talking about sending us to a civilian internment camp.

In my slow recovery from my illness, I slept much of the time. Disturbing dreams haunted me.

The *Houston* is on the bottom of the ocean! Johnny's dead!

I've gotta' get up! Miss Redecker thinks I'm goldbricking!

No! Don't drop bombs on us! No, no, no, no!

Suddenly I was awakened by a kiss, and there was Paul, feigning a defensive position to ward off a possible swinging fist.

Paul was Santa Scholastica's one bright light for me. He helped me to see the funny side of situations, no matter how depressing they were.

"What's going on?" I asked, and he mimicked the young guards' expressions when they sniffed at his bar of Palm Olive soap. Then he told me about their amazement as they watched him shave, and funnier still was his story about the one who took his fountain pen, and his explosive reaction when it leaked all over his uniform. He didn't tell me that he no longer had his soap or his razor, nor did he say anything about being soundly slapped. I found those things out later.

After awhile, Bobbie came in to talk about changing my diet from liquids to semisoft food, and eventually Velda's name came up. "She's taking this harder than any of us."

"Apparently so," I said. "It's so hard to talk to her these days."

"What's all this gossip about her?"

"Bobbie, you can't be taking that kind of nonsense seriously."

"Not when it's reported to the captain?"

"Beats me. She does crazy things sometimes, but I can't imagine her doing anything that would be reported to the captain."

118

After Bobbie left, I had been napping only a short while before the sound of someone's heels sharply hitting the wood flooring awakened me as Velda charged down the hallway and stormed into my room.

"If you have anything to say about me," she yelled, shaking her finger at me, "say it to my face!"

Well, what the hell was *this* all about?

10

SANTO TOMAS

On 8 March 1942, we nurses were ordered to appear in the courtyard, and while Lieutenant Tanaka coldly looked at us, his interpreter said, "He say you go to Santo Tomas Internment Camp. He also say, any questions."

"Are we *all* to go?" Miss Redecker asked.

"He say you all go," and while that may have been music to her ears, it spelled doom to me.

"Believe me," Paul said, "you'll be better off over there." But I couldn't see any advantage whatever in it.

On the following morning, out the gate went two trucks loaded with our trunks, beds, mattresses, pillows, linens, luggage, buckets, pots, pans, eating implements, the iron and ironing board, the sewing machine, canned goods, powdered milk, and more. Around 1300 hours, an open-air bus showed up. Miss Redecker was wearing a lei of sorts. Bobbie whispered to me, "She has all our service records stuffed into her uniform, as though that's a matter of life or death!"

It wasn't easy to say good-bye to our patients.

"Morse, I'm counting on you to keep an eye on these corpsmen," I said.

"Yes, ma'am," he answered with a big grin, and the corpsmen threatened to put him in irons if he got sassy.

"Hang onto this, will you?" Paul said, tucking his lightweight jacket over my arm. "Some of these baggy-pants have been eyeing it."

"Sure. I'll take good care of it."

"Keep in touch."

"I'll give you a jingle as soon as we get settled."

Clowning was one thing, but the only redeeming feature about going out the gate was seeing the other side of the wall. It was a sweater-weather day, a harbinger of spring with glossy new leaves on the magnolia trees. Buds were beginning to open on the colorful flame trees, and flowers were springing up in surprising spots.

Conversely, it was depressing to see Japan's Rising Sun flag on the top of the government buildings where our majestic Stars and Stripes and the Philippine flag had proudly flown beside one another for so many years. The city was not the same. Gone were the spirited honking of horns and the happy Filipinos. Few of them were seen, but we couldn't miss those who were chauffeuring Japanese officials in American-made cars.

I was going to say something to Velda when we passed the Jai Alai Building, but it was no use. She wasn't talking to me anymore. If it hadn't been Bobbie who'd said something to make her so mad, who had it been? Under the weather as

I was, it really didn't matter. In fact, I thought, if that's the way she wants it, it suits me just fine.

The bus went over the Jones Bridge, one of the few bridges still standing over the Pasig River. Along its banks the modern Treasury Building was hardly recognizable and others were damaged, but the Japanese-occupied Malacañang Palace was as beautiful as ever. Columns of black smoke rising over the Bataan Peninsula were grim reminders of why we were riding this bus. "Harriet is out there," Ellen said softly. Yes she is, I thought, wondering if we should envy her or pity her.

The bus drove on through the Escolta's dismal shopping district and finally into Calle España, where the equally depressing University of Santo Tomas stood. It was fourteen hundred hours, or, to civilians, two o'clock.

I felt that a civilian internment camp would be the world's worst, especially this huge old building that stood right in the middle of an assortment of later additions. What a letdown after Santa Scholastica. On the front corners of its roof were clusters of religious soldiers in full suits of armor, and I couldn't help but wonder about whoever had designed this monstrosity. The Big House, as it was called, was ugly, with its elaborate square structure on the center of the roof, a square that looked as tall as the main building itself. Topped by a dome and a cross, it must have risen another fifty feet. The two large classrooms on either side must have been an afterthought, each positioned equidistant from the front.

A wrought-iron fence was adorned with spears that pointed skyward, and the sawali matting attached to the inside made it seem still more threatening. But even less inspiring was the assortment of dirty mattresses and blankets draped over the tall windows' sills. No doubt a sign of lice and/or bedbugs aboard.

While the bus stopped ahead of the main gate, I was able to read part of the twelve rules listed on a sign attached to the outside of the fence:

NOTICE

By the authority of the Commander-in-Chief
Imperial Japanese Forces

(1)Salute to the Japanese soldiers when you meet them.

(2) The Japanese flag should be displayed at every house's door.

(3)Every body must put the sun-rise band on the left arm.

(4)Every body should have the certificate of residence.

(5)Whenever you see Japanese soldiers you must welcome them and not escape from them. The escaper will be considered the enemy.

(6)Unless you do not tell false prices you will be payed reasonably well.

(7) You are absolutely prohibited to walk from the sun-set to the sun-rise without car-

rying lamps. The walker who has not lights will be shot by the Japanese patrolling soldiers without any warns.

(8)Don't be fooled and bewildered by false propaganda about communists bandits and Chinese.

(9)The incendiarism accidental fire and robbery will . . .

The bus jerked forward and stopped in front of the old building's tall mahogany doors. Here, three concerned-looking American men came out to greet us.

They introduced themselves as the executive committee, adding, "We had hoped you would be coming over here, but since no news was forthcoming, we have yet to find a place to house you ladies. First we must talk to our new commandant, Mr. Tsurumi. All of the women's classrooms are filled to overflow, and opening a new one may take a little time."

With this, the Big Three went into the building with them. Still not recovered from my illness, I went to sit in the shade under a tree, from where I watched a group of socializing people waiting behind a roped-off area while others fussed around. Their clothes were mismatched and wrinkled. These were people I had probably mingled with in Manila's stores. It seemed ages ago. No doubt Johnny and I had bumped into some of them on the small dance floor in Jai Alai's Skyroom, dancing to Sammy Lahr's music.

I could hear the conversation of two of the women. "Thank God we don't have to put up with Gerty anymore. Do you know where she is now?"

"I understand the committee on order's chairman temporarily put her into the little jail set aside on the third floor until they find a room that will accept her."

Imagine that, I thought, a jail within a jail. Down came the rope and the people began picking up packages or whatever had been sent in for them. One of the men seemed to be heading my way. Suddenly he was standing by my tree, saying, "I still think blushing becomes you."

"Oh, it's *you!*" We both laughed. I'd met Ben, a civilian employee at the Navy Yard, when we were both passengers on the crowded Manila-bound *San Felipe* ferry. I'd been staring absent-mindedly into space, when suddenly his amused eyes came into focus. When he passed me on the Lagaspi Landing, he said, "Blushing becomes you."

"I'll be right back," he said now with a winning smile, and, after picking up the tools he had ordered and putting them someplace, back he came.

Ben told me about how much trouble the executive committee was going to have finding a place to house us. The University of Santo Tomas belonged to the Dominican Friars, he explained, and when the Japanese had dumped some three thousand men, women, and children here, the

Friars had had quite a time trying to salvage furnishings in the sixty-two classrooms.

Ben had been with the Allied civilians in Manila who'd been rounded up and given only a few minutes to pick up enough provisions for a three-day stay. Just for while they were registered, they'd been told. "But we're still here."

James Beckman was chairman of the executive committee, selected because he had had a leading role in a businessmen's organization. Beckman had been told to organize a committee of ten men, and, under pressure, he and nine of his business associates became the executive committee, which was to be the first of many committees and subcommittees.

Ben told me all about the place, with its swimming pool that was being used as a reservoir, its gymnasium that housed male internees, its Dominican seminary and church. There was a building for the commandant's office, and a road passed between it and the modern four-storied Educational Building.

"See that group of shanties over there by the wall? That's Froggy Bottom to their owners. This group over here call theirs The Barrio, and then there's Shanty Town."

These god-awful-looking nipa shacks apparently were prized possessions! Ben went on to talk about the annex back there somewhere, where mothers with small children lived; about the university's dump along the back wall; about the vegetable garden that was under cultivation;

about the camp hospital in the Engineering Building; and about the crude outside kitchen. He said the circus tent out back was used for a dining hall, but soon it would be replaced by something more substantial.

Finally the Big Three came out of the building, and Ben walked over with me to see what was going on. Moving in was going to be hard work, I had a feeling.

"Miss Still," Miss Redecker said, "you are to stay here with our belongings while the rest of us help the work party take our things up to Room 30A."

Time passed. The trucks were gone, and sitting uncomfortably beside what was left, I watched internees lining up for chow with their cups, tin plates, and five-pound coffee cans made into buckets.

What in the world is going on in Room 30A? Why isn't someone coming back to take the rest of this inside?

At last, Olga and a couple of the men on the detail showed up.

"We've been so busy, we forgot all about you."

"Well, thanks a lot. I could have auctioned off all this stuff. Especially these stainless-steel buckets."

Carrying Paul's jacket and the nurses' sweaters, I followed the others through the massive mahogany doors and up to the second floor. The sun shone through the oval windows and down into the courtyard outside, with its robust trees and shrubs. The lawn and flower beds, though, had obviously been well trampled upon. Some of the people were now fanning the coals in their little hibachi-like clay stoves; others were already eating their meals on folding tables.

"It must have been pretty out there, once."

"Yeah," said the man carrying the sewing machine. "This is the East Patio. Same as the West Patio."

Through the windows on the wide second-floor hallway, I looked down into the patio. Open classroom doors on the other side of the hallway revealed the most unbelievable mess. Sleeping accommodations ranged from double beds, bunk beds, cots, and native bamboo bahukas to boards on blocks. Clothing and heaven only knows what else were draped over mosquito nets hanging on sagging wires strung across the rooms. Pots, pans, cans, bottles, suitcases, footlockers, and other miscellaneous junk seemed to be everywhere.

Fire Use Only pails hung here and there on the walls, and I asked, "No fire extinguishers?"

"That's it. Wouldn't have these, the way folks borrow things even when they're nailed down, but now that we've rounded out the bottoms so they don't stand upright, they don't disappear so fast. Trouble is, borrowers don't always remember to fill 'em up with water when they put them back."

"Are the halls always this crowded?"

"Wait'll it rains," he said over his shoulder, and

I followed him into the corner room, past a bridge-playing foursome and a wife patiently telling her husband about the ladies on the sewing committee who would take in the seams of both his pants and his golf shorts.

Our beds were neatly arranged in the left-hand back corner. Six were lined up on the outside wall, the other six faced them across an eighteen-inch aisle. Each two beds abutted one another, and space between them and the next two was so narrow that one practically had to go in sideways.

My two suitcases were on the only unmade bed, and I hurriedly dropped the sweaters and jacket on top of them. Sarah's bed was next to it, and I said, "For heaven's sake, with all this space, why are the beds so close together?"

"Each internee is allowed only twenty-two square feet of floor space, that's why."

"Sarah, I'm about to burst," I said, and I followed her directions down the hall, only to find long noisy lines of men and women standing outside their respective restrooms, many in robes and carrying towels. A jaunty-looking gray-haired monitor sat beside the entrance to the men's restroom, his feet propped on the side rungs of a tilted chair, handing four squares of neatly folded toilet paper to each man about to enter.

To cope with my uncomfortable situation, I diverted my attention by picking up bits of conversation.

"Howdy, Mr. Powell, never thought I'd see my bank's president passing out toilet paper."

"Bill, you know the bank has always passed out deposit slips."

The monitor for the women's restroom also passed out four sheets of toilet tissue, and once inside, I was astonished. It was wall-to-wall women and there was a deafening chicken-yard cacophony. Naked, except for one who wore panties and a bra, several women shivered under the cold-water showerheads attached to a jerry-rigged pipe extending across the length of the room.

Under a frosted window was a sign: If You Want Privacy Close Your Eyes.

At last, with my mission accomplished, I couldn't get out of there fast enough. Unfortunately I found myself in the line of fire as two women started a knock-down-and-dragout, and when I returned to Room 30A I was sopping wet.

"Good grief! What happened to you?"

"Well, do you know what I'm going to do? I'm going to write a letter to the Bureau of Medicine and Surgery and ask for a transfer to Bataan. It has to be safer out there!"

11

BATAAN FALLS

That first night in Room 30A was dreadful. As in the Jai Alai Building, sounds echoed across the almost empty room with its high ceiling. If it wasn't bed springs squeaking, Sarah's wheezing, Velda's coughing, Ellen's sniffling, or Olga's sighing, it was the guards' heavy boots shuffling along the asphalt road as they made their rounds. Shortly after midnight it was the galley crews in the three outside kitchens filling cauldrons with water and stacking logs under them, and after that, with the smell of coffee brewing, who could sleep?

The next day our neat little corner was hidden as the room filled up with a great variety of women. There were single and married women, mothers with teenage daughters, older women, one overly aggressive missionary whose joy was leaving religious literature on everyone's bed.

At least Gerty was out of jail. Her attitude and gaudy manner of dress flaunted her profession. She seemed to have a sisterly attitude toward Matilda, who bedded next to her, and I must say their combined floor space was neater than most.

We decided that the comically bow-legged, friendly, but not so bright Russian should have had more limeade and sunshine as a child.

Martha, the room monitor, gave each of us a punch-out meal ticket for March, and we laughed at "Compliments of Pabst Blue Ribbon Beer" printed on the back. Nothing like advertising, we thought.

Personality conflicts were inevitable, of course. Room 30A was better than some, not as good as others. Differences of opinion in our corner were handled in a quiet Navy Nurse Corps manner. For instance, Julia had intended to put Miss Redecker's suitcases on the bed farthest back because of the privacy it afforded, if you could call it that. Liz had already made up the bed for herself, and Miss Redecker told Julia to let it go. "In this internment camp rank has no priority, anyway," someone added.

Despite some grumbling it was soon a buried issue, but there was worse when Miss Redecker went right over to the camp's hospital. Not only did she take over as the director of nurses, she offered our services as well! "Ladies," she said frostily, "you are not forced to work in this internment camp, but if you do not want to do nursing, you may clean vegetables, sort weevils and rocks out of the rice, or monitor the bathrooms, but you *will do* something." And that was an order.

Already Filipino doctors and nurses had been allowed to come in to help, and the MaryKnoll nursing sisters handled the night shift. We soon found out why no one was asked to work longer than two to four hours a day. Who could when so much of one's time was spent standing in lines?

There were lines for the restroom, lines for washing one's hair outside under one of two showerheads attached to a water pipe over a propped-up bathtub, lines for rinsing dishes or washing one's laundry under one of many faucets strung along a pipe over a crude trough. And of course one never hung laundry out to dry unguarded.

Naturally the chow line was the longest, and who were the wiseacres who posted menus such as this at the serving table?

Roast beef
Potatoes au gratin
Tossed green salad
Apple pie
Coffee Tea Milk

In the evenings we could listen to music broadcast over a PA system, attend concerts put on by the camp's musicians, or, on occasion, take in a Sammy Lahr stage show, now that the stage had been built.

Like everyone else who was waiting for the American forces to come back, we fell for outlandish rumors and doubted the truth. We scoffed at the *Manila Tribune*'s propaganda, when we could find one of the two copies that were

133

distributed daily to each classroom.

"Isn't this a scream? It says here the Japanese Navy sank the U.S. Navy Department!" There were headlines such as CALIFORNIA SHORES SHELLED, JAPAN PREPARED TO WAGE WAR FOR A HUNDRED YEARS, and FDR STATES THAT AMERICAN SHORES CANNOT BE DEFENDED.

More logical were the whispered reports, which we got either through the grapevine or from hidden radios: Japan's navy is paying heavily for every inch it sails; Japan's army is taking a beating in a big battle in Cebu; our boys on Bataan were pushing forward. These reports *had* to be true.

True or not, rumors were the camp's lifeblood. No one doubted that the American forces would be back; it was just a matter of when. Next week? Next month? Less encouraging were newspaper stories about how General MacArthur had deserted his men and the Filipinos. Could that be? Tokyo Rose said, "What a shame. Your great master MacArthur has left you in the lurch."

Through the Filipino nurses we learned that the general had left the Philippines because he had been ordered to, but despite all the secrecy involved in getting him to Australia, Tokyo Rose reported, "He'll never make it."

He did make it, though, and his "I shall return!" message came through to us clearly.

Chilling were the stories told by individuals or families who had no longer been able to hide out in the mountains, people who'd spent days subjected to terrifying interrogations in Fort Santiago's dank dungeons. Firsthand evidence of real Japanese cruelty came via the former owner of the *Manila Tribune*. He had been in Santo Tomas since the Japanese occupation and was so broken in spirit that he was afraid to speak, and his once dark hair had turned white.

Life could be very grim if one dwelt on sordid stories like these. The thought of dying didn't bother me as much as living with guilt, and according to the catechism books, for my many sins I could expect the worst. Cursing Johnny and the *Houston* had to be a mortal sin punishable by eternal damnation, but was there really a heaven and a hell? Was there life after death? I just didn't know.

Most of the religious orders, Catholic and Protestant, had been allowed to remain in their outside establishments, but some of the Protestant ministers and their families were in Santo Tomas. Recently a fatherly Irish priest was allowed to hold mass under the trees out front, and Bobbie and I attended Sunday masses with our Catholic nurses.

Father O'Leary and Liz got along famously, the two of them always having something to say to one another, but to Bobbie and me, his " 'tis welcome you are" reminded us that " 'Tis many a convert that will be at the communion rail two weeks from today."

Should I or shouldn't I? I wanted to be able to pray and receive God's graces, but on the other hand, while lessons in some of the biblical parables were as easy to understand as Aesop's Fables, some of the things the Catholics believed on faith alone seemed unreasonable.

No, this is not for me, I decided again. As Easter drew closer, ominous rumors about the war had a ring of truth to them, I thought. The *Houston* could be on the bottom of the ocean, Johnny could be dead, and if so, it was all my fault.

God, can You forgive me? If I become a Catholic, will You hear me? Can I accept the faith tongue-in-cheek and hope it will all become clear in time? Can I unload my wicked soul to a confessor? Oh, no, I can't do that.

As though to help me decide, the *Manila Tribune* was filled with terrible things about Bataan. Were they trying to demoralize the civilians? Of course, they were, but what if they weren't? Was morale really as low among our forces out there as they were saying it was?

It was all too much for me to handle alone and, on Holy Saturday, Bobbie and I stood in the long line of nervous internees waiting to face the humiliating experience of exposing our sinful souls to another human being for the first time in our lives.

On 5 April, Easter Sunday, with Lizzy as our godmother, the two of us were among the camp's many new Catholics receiving their first communion. My heavy burden of guilt was gone, and I knew God would now hear my prayers. I was at peace with myself and with God, and if I were destined to die young, I was ready.

We were jeered by some, but this new feeling of belonging and self-worth was too important to be rent asunder, I thought, by these men or by anyone else. Not now, not ever.

Across town only the tuberculosis patients, an attending doctor, several corpsmen, and three captains remained at Santa Scholastica. They listened to the German sisters sing, watched them work in their vegetable garden, and looked at Japanese planes flying overhead. Not much fun, but we heard that by using the Navy's welfare funds, Captain Boyle was able to provide a special fried-chicken dinner, complete with ice cream for dessert.

Those at Pasay were not so fortunate. We complained about twenty-two square feet of floor space in Room 30A, but at Pasay only senior officers had thin mattresses between them and the cement floor. For the rest, it was sixty men in classrooms built for thirty elementary students. More captured soldiers were brought in each day, and many prisoners slept outside on the dirt.

While we stood in tediously long chow lines for monotonous mush and coffee for breakfast, mongo beans for lunch, and rice and stew with sometimes a banana for dinner, at Pasay the twice-a-day rations were tasteless soup with some rice that had been cooked into a pasty consistency known to the natives as lugao.

While we shivered under cold showers, Pasay

had only one outside faucet with a showerhead attached higher up, and water shortage limited its use. While we had a reasonable amount of donated or privately bought medicine to treat our patients, at Pasay medicine bottles filled with colored water on the shelves of a bookcase were humorously meant to convey the impression of a real clinic.

The medical staff could do little for the sick and injured, but, in keeping with the Navy's promotional program, corpsmen with sufficient longevity in the service studied toward upgrading their ratings. Whether the Hospital Corps in Washington would recognize such advancements was not as important as the mental exercise it gave the involved officers and corpsmen alike.

At 1:30 A.M., 9 April, a strong earthquake shook the Big House. Pots, pans, tin cans, and all else went bouncing over the floor. Crisscrossing wires snapped, and pandemonium reigned. But it would turn out to be our armed forces on Bataan that were in a state of collapse, not this sturdy old building.

When daylight finally came, the guards were out there doing their seven o'clock calisthenics as usual, while the camp's strategists pondered the question of which way the American forces would come into the city.

BATAAN HAS FALLEN, the *Manila Tribune* reported. That couldn't be, but a solemn voice on the PA system said Mr. Itoshi had informed

138

the executive committee that it was indeed so. But was the commandant telling us the truth?

The next day's paper left no doubt. Pictured was a Japanese general seated at a table between Major General King and another high-ranking U.S. Army officer with two armed Japanese soldiers standing behind them. For days thereafter, starved and heartsick civilians were brought into Santo Tomas, women mostly, wives, some with children, and we learned some of the hard facts about warfare on the peninsula. They cried as they recalled the horrible conditions they had somehow survived and how the sick and starved servicemen had hardly had enough strength to fight, even if there had been enough ammunition.

"An army travels on its stomach" is an old truism, and, for hundreds of our American and Filipino soldiers, starvation had been as fatal as the enemy's bullets and bombs. Foraging civilians had helped deplete the countryside, right down to the last jack rabbit. Uncontrollable filth had contaminated the rivers and streams, and hundreds of disease-stricken soldiers had died unattended.

Distorted rumors left us ignorant of what was going on, but we eagerly hung onto whatever information came our way. I learned that with the fall of Bataan imminent, the captain and crew of the *Canopus* had prepared to join the Marines on Corregidor's Monkey Point. Because the ship was so badly damaged when it was ordered to hide out in the Mariveles Harbor, its captain had it tilted at a grotesque angle and had oily rags smoldering for days to fool the enemy. The channel was so heavily mined that the *Canopus* could no longer function as a submarine tender, but PT boat captains and the Army soon discovered that the mechanics could build anything from bolts to engines.

They repaired the *Canopus* well enough to sail her into the deep water under her own power, and then down she went in a blaze of glory. After salvaging as much fuel and ammunition as possible from the volcanic hillside tunnels, the captain and crew dynamited the entrances to seal off the rest. Then they scrambled aboard whatever was available to take them to Corregidor. The hillside became a blazing inferno as exploding gasoline drums ignited the torpedoes and whatever else had been left.

Grace, one of the women who came into Santo Tomas, told us she had helped the nurses in the Army's two field hospitals. She had been there, she said, during the final hours of 8 April, when General Jonathan Wainwright had ordered the nurses in both Hospital #1 (where Harriet was) and Hospital #2 (farther down on the peninsula) to leave for Corregidor. One of the senior Army nurses had apparently refused to go without Grace and the Filipino nurses, but Grace had decided to stay anyway. She wanted to find her husband.

At Santa Scholastica in its closing days, the

tuberculosis patients were sent to a local TB sanitarium and the three captains to a camp in Tarlac for high-ranking officers, leaving Dr. Kleinfeldt and the corpsmen to wrap up loose ends. Lieutenant Tanaka stopped to chat with the doctor, in perfect English. In a friendly man-to-man visit, they casually talked about personal interests such as schooling, careers, likes and dislikes, homes and families. When Dr. Kleinfeldt said his family was in Long Beach, California, Tanaka sympathetically said, "Oh, too bad. That city has been destroyed."

In other military camp developments, the former Pasay Elementary School was renamed Japanese Accommodation Place, a storehouse for slave labor, and we discovered through the grapevine that our medical staff and patients had been transferred to the old Bilibid Prison, hardly more than a stone's throw from Santo Tomas.

Captain Kusomoto, an Imperial navy doctor, put Commander Stewart in charge of the medical unit in this wreck of a partially dismantled prison, which had been replaced by the New Bilibid Prison near Muntinlupa. The old prison afforded space — if nothing else it was better than Pasay — but for a hospital, it would take a lot of effort and ingenuity on the part of our Navy men to make it reasonably livable.

12

CORREGIDOR FALLS

BOMBS DEMOLISH CORREGIDOR GUNS, reported the *Tribune* on 15 April, and the newspaper went on at great length about how General Homma's forces were battering the rock island. This we didn't want to believe, but we would later know that they really were, hour after hour, day after day. It would take three weeks to silence Corregidor's guns, as one by one its retractable cannons and battery emplacements were bombed out. Fort Drum kept up a continual barrage along its southern exposure, and the old *Idaho*'s big guns would have the distinction of firing the last shells.

We would also learn that artillery shells from Bataan had at least given the men on Monkey Point's beach a chance to jump into their foxholes, but bombs from farther out gave no forewarning. Lucky were the former Shanghai Marines, whose four-legged Corporal Soochow could hear Japanese aircraft as soon as they took off from Clark Field: heeding his reactions had given them a fighting chance to see another day. There could be no tears for lost buddies, a phenomenon that had already become a way of life. No tears, at least for now.

On Corregidor proper, the hospital had long since been moved from the topside down into the maze of Malinta's stuffy, dusty tunnels. Bunks in tiers of three replaced hospital beds, and twenty-four-hour pounding brought in waves of casualties, so many that the nurses and corpsmen took on emergency tasks ordinarily handled by the doctors.

MacArthur ordered two PBYs to Corregidor to fly out key personnel, filling the remaining passenger space at General Wainwright's discretion. It was not an easy choice, but on 29 April nineteen Army nurses were among those who left the island fortress.

A nighttime rendezvous with the submarine *Spearfish* had been arranged, a last chance for anyone to leave the doomed island. The captain of the *Canopus*, Harriet, and eleven Army nurses were among the selected twenty-four passengers. We would learn that it was they who bobbed along in a motor launch, wondering if the submarine could penetrate the patrolling Japanese destroyers. It was they who saw the flashing bombs burst as parts of Corregidor's cliff gave way; they who sighed with relief when the conning tower of the submarine surfaced. Then, as if a finale to this horrifying spectacle, flights of bombers struck with such force that flames seemed to engulf the entire island.

On the following day, with Corregidor's remaining guns still blazing, heavy enemy tanks came ashore and gained entrance to the Malinta tunnels. On 6 May, up went the white flag.

On 7 May, the *Manila Tribune*'s headline read JAPANESE FORCES NEAR COMPLETE MASTERY, and on 8 May, CORREGIDOR FALLS. A full-page spread left no room for doubt: pictured was General Wainwright flanked by Japanese officers, his head bowed, a microphone on the table in front of him.

On the next day, WAINWRIGHT ORDERS ENTIRE USAFFE SURRENDER, but through the "bamboo telegraph" I also heard that a number of servicemen and officers had headed for the hills to join the growing number of guerrilla bands. Japan's additional ten thousand prisoners on Corregidor waited anxiously for what would happen next, and on the same day, hundreds of American and Filipino prisoners began the infamous Death March of Bataan.

This issue also pictured a beaming General Homma in a parade, with Filipinos applauding enthusiastically as he made his triumphal entry into the city of Manila. "They were applauding because their band was playing 'God Bless America' in a lively marching tempo," Rick joked.

Taller than most and handsome in their white dress uniforms, Captain Kusomoto and two other Imperial navy doctors came to visit Santo Tomas, and especially to see us nurses. Because of their disarming attitude, using her VIP accent, Miss

Redecker gave them a tour of the camp's hospital. In turn, they gave us regards from Dr. Stewart and some of our other doctors. We answered their questions about our nursing careers, and from them we learned that the Japanese military didn't have a female nurse corps. They also told us that our Navy men were doing quite well, but from notes passed back and forth, we got a better idea of what the huge prison compound of Bilibid was really like. It would turn out to be even worse than we could have imagined.

Most of the plumbing and wiring were gone, and rust left holes in the corrugated iron roof. Piles of trash made fine breeding grounds for flies, snakes, and rats. On the lower lever, what was designated the Japanese Hospital for Military Prisoner of War Camps was in reasonably good shape by now, considering what our former maintenance crew had to work with. The upper level, like Pasay, was another Japanese Accommodation Place on a grander scale, where prisoners from outlying camps were brought in before being sent out on work parties. When 1,500 came in, 1,500 went out, and the dead-on-arrival and the dying or acutely ill were replaced by recovering patients. The doctors soon realized that by signing a patient's release, they could be signing his death warrant.

Captain Kusomoto offered death injections for worthless people like Jeffery Morse and permanent cripples, but Dr. Stewart told him that would violate the Hippocratic oath American

145

physicians honored and lived by. Kusomoto respected this.

Bornowski's daily log on 3 July 1942 reads:

J. Garcia, Corporal, Medical Department, PI Army, died at 2248 this date. Cause of death: Malaria, Malignant, Tertian. Buried in row two, grave 24. Seventy-two Filipino patients discharged to their homes. Dysentery ward moved to old cell blocks in buildings 16 and 17 for better isolation. Patient census: 808.

Here in Santo Tomas, before one of the MaryKnoll sisters went off night duty, she handed me a crumpled note from a deep pocket in her habit. It was from Paul. We already knew about shutterbugs among the Japanese guards; several of them had taken pictures here in Santo Tomas. Paul said he had talked one of them into taking a picture of us nurses. "When he wanted to know why we called him Mortimer Snerd, we said it was because he reminded us of a famous movie star. You should have seen him strut!"

I didn't tell Miss Redecker or the others about this, and she was especially annoyed when we were told to come over to the front of the Big House. There he was, a living replica of Edgar Bergen's dummy! Click, click, went his camera, and with a smiling "Tank'cu. Tank'cu," he left. On this same roll of film, he'd already taken two other pictures: Captain Kusomoto with Paul, and another warrant officer with a corpsman. By some hook or crook, a contact print of these two snapshots showed up for me!

As in Bilibid, Santo Tomas settled into a day-by-day existence, waiting for the American forces to come back. We nurses in Room 30A were polite and friendly enough, but we didn't have enough in common to make close friends with the other internees, and we did not go out of our way to do so.

Gerty and Matilda were a couple of my favorites because they had such colorful characters. Whether she was working as a restroom monitor, sorting weevils and gravel out of rice, or cleaning vegetables, Gerty was always dressed in high heels, flashy clothes, and lacy gloves.

We all felt that it would probably take a few months more before our forces would be back, and shanty towns had a strong appeal for those who could afford them. A source of pride for their owners, the little suburbs even had mayors, councilmen, district supervisors, building codes, and streets with catchy names. Each shack was different in design. In conformance with a Japanese rule, they had to be open on two sides. Still, they provided protection from the sun and inclement weather, gave a measure of privacy, and they were a place to socialize and gloat about the beauty of their owners' morning-glory vines and flower beds.

Of course, these were for the "haves," not the "have-nots." But the haves did have consciences, pointing out that since their food was brought in, the chow line could offer more for the less fortunate.

And, for those who could afford it, chow-line rice, mush, and mongo beans could be enhanced by adding duck eggs and whatever other strange ingredients came in with the Filipino merchants.

Because it was impossible for the on-duty staff to stand in the long chow lines, eating in the hospital kitchen was an accepted practice. Dietitian-prepared food for a hundred or so people made a world of difference. Here the windows were screened, and if ordinary flies or their bluebottle cousins gained entry, they were doomed by the janitorial executioners. With advantages like these, we didn't mind working extra hours.

I thought it was silly not to eat the main kitchen's lunches, though. Mongo beans weren't that bad, but this was another one of Liz's I'll-die-first items, and they were too fattening for Olga.

In mid July, Lizzy mentioned how nice it would be to have a chocolate cake like the ones her mother had always made for her on her birthday. Long ago she had learned how to manipulate people without seeming to do so, much to Olga's disapproval. Her lively chatter and infectious laughter won her the friendship of an amused internee couple who chose to be victimized, and they enjoyed Liz's game as much as she did.

Naturally, the cakes were shared with the rest of us.

Later that month, the pending arrival of about sixty or seventy Army nurses immediately had tongues wagging. Felicia said Harriet could have her bed: she would have a native bahuka bed brought in for herself. But Miss Redecker said we would have to think of something else.

We had their rooms ready on time, but it was several days before a parade of trucks came through the gate. In a matter of minutes, the Army nurses were overwhelmed as applauding internees crowded around them, shouting as they recognized someone they knew. But the guards pushed them back.

"Geez, they sure look bushed," Joyce said.

"Looks as though they need showers, clean clothes, and plenty of rest," Bobbie observed.

But where was Harriet? Suddenly I shouted, "Doris! Doris Delaney!" and pushed my way toward the front of the crowd.

"Dottie? Dottie Still? Is that really you?" But before we could say anything else, the guards pushed everyone back.

"Who's that?"

"A nursing-school classmate. I didn't know her too well, but she's the last one I would expect to see in the Army Nurse Corps."

Surprisingly, instead of taking these women to the cleaned classrooms, the guards hustled them back onto the trucks. Out the front gate they went, but no farther away than the Santa Catalina convent across the street on the east side, there to be isolated from the camp.

As a medium of exchange, British pounds, Netherlands guilders, U.S. dollars, and gold-backed Philippine pesos were useless. The Japanese printed pesos and different levels of centavoes by the billions to replace them, and naturally enough, outsiders gladly salted away good currency for this Mickey Mouse scrip.

There were places within the camp to spend it. Employees from Aguinaldo's Department Store came in to take orders, a Japanese couple had a coffee shop, and enterprising internees bought outside baked goods for resale in the camp. Others made and sold candy. Barbers, beauticians, and dressmakers built up their own clienteles, but except for services, it took money to make money, and that we nurses didn't have.

Velda, however, got the required license for her Anchor Lending Library, and, with donated books, she set up a table in the hallway. Liz, Ellen, Joyce, and Olga sat in for her when she was on duty or on the sick list, which was often. I mended torn books, hoping to improve our strained relationship, but it didn't work.

But Velda's entrepreneurship soon died from internal conflict. "Dottie, look at this!" Lizzy said one day, laughing. "And this isn't the first complaint she's pinned to my pillow."

There were bad days and good. It was always depressing to hear the Filipino nurses say, "They are very mean to our people. They tie some of them to lamp posts and leave them there to die." Or, "Some say too much. Now they have no tongues. Ah, many, many fine Philippine Scouts die at Camp O'Donnell."

There were bright moments, even with the Japanese. Santo Tomas youngsters loved to race ahead of patrolling guards and bow. The guards would stop, click their heels, bow politely, and then the youngsters would run ahead to repeat the same ritual.

"Honestly, those kids are asking for trouble," I said to no one in particular one day.

"No need to worry, Miss Still." Since almost everyone called me Dottie, I looked up suspiciously at this fellow. "The guards like to play games with them. Why, ma'am, some of the ranking officers take them outside for ice cream cones and candy treats."

"Yeah? But don't I know you from somewhere?"

"Yes ma'am," he said with a big grin, and whispered, "Sergeant Costello, 4th Marine Corps. I was a patient at the San Diego Navy Hospital."

"Of course!" I answered quietly. "I remember you. My word, you jumped from a private to a sergeant in a hurry. When did you get out of the service?"

"Ma'am, I haven't been discharged," he whispered. "Didn't get out of Manila in time. Gave my name, rate, and serial number when the Nips picked me up. Guess they didn't know what else

151

to do with me, an' like Pa would say, it's best to let sleepin' dogs lie."

Over the months of bunking next to her, I got to know Sarah so well that her nightly wheezing went unheard. On this night, however, her labored breathing was different. "Sarah, are you all right?"

"I can hardly breathe," she said, and I could see her propped up on her pillow, grimacing painfully, running her hand over the left side of her chest, and I rushed over to look for her medications.

"This isn't emphysema," she moaned.

A heart attack, I thought, and ran over to alert Miss Redecker. Both she and Julia were at Sarah's bedside in seconds, and off to the hospital the three of them went.

Go back to bed, Miss Redecker had said. A lot of good that would do. So with my rosary in one pocket and cigarettes and matches in another, I went into the hallway where chronic insomniacs visited quietly. Since it would have been improper to smoke a cigarette and say the rosary at the same time, I lit a cigarette and sat down on the top of the stairwell.

"May I have a light?" a voice whispered.

Sitting beside me, my new friend Helen and I talked about our worries. She was having a hard time making a decision. She had a chance to leave, but she wasn't sure she should. Her husband, John, said he wouldn't even hesitate, but if she wasn't comfortable about it, they wouldn't go.

"It's an exchange of diplomats and civilians?"

"That's what they say. We were told we'd be taken to Shanghai, and from there to a neutral port in India where a repatriation would be made."

"Oh, Helen, this is one chance in a million."

"But it's so frightening, with the war going on out there."

We talked until we were relaxed enough to go back to bed, by which time she had talked herself into going.

In the morning Sarah was on her way to an outside hospital, diagnosed as having had a not-too-severe heart attack. She was back within two weeks. Still, it had been a warning. "I'm not dying! Quit fussing over me," she would say indignantly.

On the departure day for Shanghai-bound internees, I went down to wish Helen and John a safe trip. The Big Three and Clara were there to say good-bye to two Canadian couples, and once back in Room 30A, Miss Redecker announced, "Ladies, we own a shanty."

The days passed by. Critically ill and surgical patients were sent to outside hospitals while we doled out emetine, carbasone, bismuth, or paregoric to patients with dysentery and nonspecific diarrhea. We administered the new sulfonamides for infections. We shaved lice-infested heads and painted them with potassium permanganate; scabies lesions with gentian violet. Then, as though perpetrated by an angry God, an amoebic dysentery epidemic struck with a vengeance.

The commandant notified Major Sikiguchi, assistant chief of medicine in the Philippines. That doctor wanted to know why the Americans needed interpreters when the Japanese learned the languages of the people wherever they went. And why couldn't the great American doctors control an epidemic? Japanese doctors could.

Stool specimens were to be taken on everyone, and lab reports were due within a week. No one blamed Dr. Lloyd for quitting after the lashing he took from the "Wicked Major Siki," as he called himself.

Joyce volunteered to work long hours with the lab technician. "I don't mind," she said. "I've done lab work before."

Carriers were soon discovered among the main kitchen crew, and once this was under control, no new cases developed. Even though these men worked harder and longer than most, getting replacements presented no problem whatever. In fact, the merchant seamen had created a closed shop in the main kitchen, where they had easy access to the food supplies. Pilfering, yes, but moving the heavy cawas from the kitchen to the serving area was a back-breaking job, and no one complained.

The camp's housing problems worsened as

more people came in, and again the commandant took the executive committee out into the country to look at other sites that might be suitable for relocating the camp. Nothing was found, but with the increased patient load, the executive committee decided to rent the Santa Catalina convent with camp funds. The Army nurses would move into the Engineering Building, and the convent would be the hospital. Rested but tired of being isolated, the Army nurses wanted access to the main campus while retaining the dormitory's privacy. Nevertheless, they had to move.

"I didn't join the Army Nurse Corps to take care of civilians," some mumbled. As far as I was concerned, this was the same song, second verse.

Moving kept them busy, but Doris and I at least had a chance to say a few passing words, although plans for a good visit got no further than fleeting conversations. Miss Redecker turned over her supervisory position to Army Captain Crawford with her much larger nurse corps. That was as it should be, although when the two-week work schedule was posted, the civilian and Navy nurses' names did not appear. It wasn't long before that oversight was corrected; we forgotten nurses assumed Miss Redecker had been employing her icy-eyed foot-stomping.

There was no similarity between her and her Army counterpart other than their commanding positions. Both were conscientious leaders and neither would allow herself to be stepped on. But the manner in which each accomplished this differed considerably. Miss Redecker made her presence known in her quiet, defiant way, while Captain Crawford had an authoritative desk-pounding approach.

She reminded us Navy nurses of a bellowing bosun's mate, while the Army nurses probably considered Miss Redecker a gutless wonder. In time, though, our two groups got to know one another better. They were as deep-cored Army as we were Navy. They were friendly enough superficially, but we felt we were merely being tolerated.

Oh, well. They got the Army mule, but *we* got the Marines!

13

LIFE IN SANTO TOMAS

The shanty should have been our nurses' castle, but it wasn't. It was nicer than most, with built-in cupboards to store our shared pots and pans. Its picnic table was large enough for all of us to eat our meals together, but only when Lizzy had a birthday cake did we gather there.

"It's Miss Redecker's shanty," was the general attitude and, except for the Big Three and me, the others used it only when the chief nurse wasn't there. She said it was for all of us, and I took her at her word. I wasn't about to balance a plate of food on my bed or put up with clouds of flies in the dining shed. Not if I didn't have to.

I tried to eat early and leave before the Big Three arrived. This wasn't always possible, and sitting discreetly at the other end of the table, I got to know our chief nurse better.

"Lucille," Sarah said one day, "I wonder if we're not the first American Navy nurses ever to be taken prisoners of war."

"Possibly not; it is no doubt true that Guam fell. I sincerely hope the five nurses there were

157

sent out ahead of time, but perhaps not."

This subject exhausted, Julia put in, "Oh, heavenly day, I expect the Bureau is going crazy. Can you imagine how many nurses are being inducted into the service?"

"I do not envy Sue Dauser," Miss Redecker said. "It must be very difficult to be the superintendent of the Nurse Corps at a time like this." Then she added, "Imagine what it would be like if one-tenth of one percent of these nurses were Dorothys."

"Miss Redecker!" Julia said, joining in.

"Do you know you'll be a heroine when you return to the mainland?" Miss Redecker said to me then.

"For being here? You've got to be joking! You all better stop picking on me or I won't be a fourth at your bridge game when you can't find anyone else."

"Big loss!" Sarah said, and we all broke into peals of laughter.

As one might expect, politics played a part in the internal affairs at Santo Tomas. Obviously there were more Americans here than any of the other Allied nationalities. Possibly one-fourth were British, Australians, and Canadians; a sprinkling of Dutch and a few others comprised the rest. It was an American executive committee, and there were American committee chairmen down the line. Perhaps this was because the English block had taken a wait-and-see attitude, vol-

*The author in 1935, as a student nurse at the
Los Angeles General County Hospital.*

Above: *First tour of duty: outside the San Diego Naval Hospital Contagion Ward.*

Right: *The miniature lighthouses along the seawall at the Cañacao Naval Hospital compound, Cavite, the Philippines. Sangley Point is in the background.*

The Cañacao Naval Hospital
administration building, 1940.

*The nurses quarters at the
Cañacao Naval Hospital, 1940.*

The commanding officer's quarters
at the Cañacao Naval Hospital.

The Navy nurses interned at Santo Tomas, September 1942.
The author is in the second row, at far right. The photograph
was taken by one of the Japanese guards.
(Courtesy of the Bureau of Medicine and Surgery Archives)

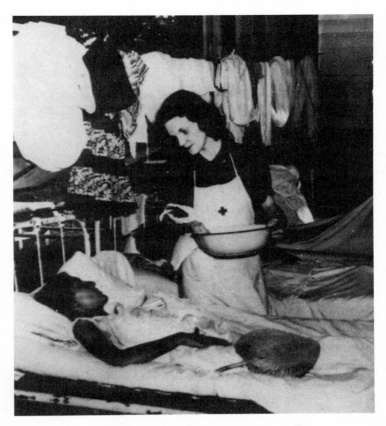

Above: *Nurse Elizabeth Moran attends to a patient in Santo Tomas.* (Courtesy of the Bureau of Medicine and Surgery Archives)

Left: *Internees washing their hair in Santo Tomas.* (Courtesy of the Bureau of Medicine and Surgery Archives)

The nurses liberated from Los Baños being briefed by Admiral Thomas C. Kinkaid. The author, suffering from extreme exhaustion, is seated at left. (Courtesy of the Bureau of Medicine and Surgery Archives)

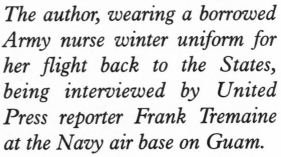

The author, wearing a borrowed Army nurse winter uniform for her flight back to the States, being interviewed by United Press reporter Frank Tremaine at the Navy air base on Guam.

Lt. Dorothy Still in 1945.

unteering for very little, yet doing their share of the workload.

After all these boring months (it was now almost Fall), we began to hear complaints about the executive committee's having been appointed. It didn't really represent the internee body, it was said. The English block felt they were not being represented at all. As a result of all this, Mr. Beckman asked the commandant's permission to hold an election.

Mr. Tsurumi said he would appoint a new committee, but Mr. Beckman explained it wasn't that he or any of the other members wanted to quit. The problem was that the people wanted an elected committee, not another appointed one. Weeks later, the vacillating commandant gave his approval.

An election was slated for 24 August, and delegates from each room nominated candidates who electioneered diligently. Beckman and most of his committee were voted out and Ray Sackett was voted in as chairman. Then, on 1 September, Mr. Tsurumi announced his retirement.

Mr. Kodaki, chief of the Japanese Department of External Affairs, became the new commandant. He retained this position, and his assistant, Mr. Kuroda, more often than not was the acting commandant. Kodaki had studied in America, England, and France, and knew Westerners well. Kuroda, a businessman in China, imported Western-made merchandise. Younger than previous commandants, they both spoke English.

Meanwhile, the new executive committee joyfully jumped into its role. Beckman's committee had successfully dealt with the perplexing rules of the changing commandants and had managed camp affairs prudently; one of its victories had been gaining the use of a small room in the Big House for a jail. This kept camp drunkards and other offenders out of sight and out of military hands.

The new committee, though, seemed to miss the importance of mediating between the Japanese and the internees. They moved the jail into the small building behind the commandant's office, which was distressing enough, but why did they have to broadcast the names and offenses of lawbreakers over the PA system?

Equally unfortunate was a new law allowing room occupants to vote out unacceptable roommates. For this and similar reasons, several monitors and committee chairmen quit.

While members of the new regime were making their irritating rules and regulations, Mr. Kodaki compiled his Nine Rules. He firmly stated that those who disobeyed camp rules would make his relations with the military so difficult that he planned to submit full reports on all offenders to them for sentencing.

Rules related to the Package Line had been ignored, and internees were not being kept at the prescribed distance from the shed. Uncensored or poorly censored notes had been found in both incoming and outgoing packages, the efforts of internees and their Filipino friends to communicate. Kodaki had the operation shut down, which could have crippled the camp's resources had not Mr. Beckman stepped in. Fortunately he had been retained in an advisory status, and he got Kodaki to accept a sawali fence around the shed.

General discontent prompted "town hall meetings" in an effort to iron out differences. A protestant minister chaired the organization. The primary objectives were first to make the internees aware of the executive committee's imposed limitations, second, to review past accomplishments, and third, to set goals for the future. The first meeting generated considerable interest and enthusiasm, but then something went wrong.

Sackett thought Kodaki should be told what the large gathering was all about before it was brought to his attention through other sources. The result was that Kodaki created a new rule: no unauthorized assemblies. All classroom lessons, church sermons, any gathering had to be approved by the commandant's office.

And then Kodaki surprised us when he invited the internees to assemble in the Father's Garden to hear a guest speaker, a distinguished Japanese gentleman. "Mr. Izzawa has recently returned from the United States," Kodaki said in introducing him. Pleased to see such a big turnout, he told us about the deprivations and maltreatment both his guest and his fellow countrymen had been subjected to before they had been repatriated. "By knowing these facts," Kodaki said, "you will be able to appreciate the benevolence of the Emperor of Japan."

Neatly dressed in a Western-style suit, Mr. Izzawa arose and bowed to our polite applause. He told us that, as the "chargé d'affaires" in Panama, he and the other members of the Japanese embassy staff had been herded out of their quarters and flown to the White Sulfur Springs Hotel in West Virginia, where they had been forced to remain for a long time.

"Wow! That's one of the swankiest resorts in the whole country!" was quietly whispered, and nothing Izzawa said convinced us that he'd had it worse than we did in this civilian internment camp.

"I'm actually embarrassed for Mr. Kodaki," Bobbie whispered, and the longer Izzawa talked, the more Kodaki visibly squirmed, especially when his guest ended by asking if there were any questions. One or two polite and innocuous inquiries were made, and the assembly was quickly dismissed.

"Geez, the nasty Americans probably took away his golf clubs!"

"Imagine having nothing better than leftover roast beef for lunch!"

Mr. Izzawa had obviously addressed the wrong audience. The plight of the uprooted and mistreated Japanese-American citizens along the California coast may have been more comparable to ours. They too had lost their land and their hard-earned possessions. Among the young Japanese-American men who returned to Japan to join the military were some recognized by our POWs as being former classmates — "the meanest bastards ever," they were called.

We talked about Izzawa's speech for days. Firsthand news from the States, we joked, and, as if to get our minds on something else, a bonus movie was brought in.

Even better than the movie was the propaganda film that preceded it. This showed hundreds of dressed-alike Japanese citizens participating in mass exercises. Then there were scenes from a sports event and, as a finale, torch bearers led a parade. The camera zoomed in on one of the torches, whose flame covered the entire screen.

One could escape temporarily from this boring existence by getting lost in a book, and under the loneliest tree I could find, I was well into the second chapter of *Green Acres* by Lloyd Douglas before I was interrupted. "You look much too comfortable," Doris said, sitting down.

Green Acres could wait, I decided; I'd been wanting to ask Doris about how she'd happened to join the Army Nurse Corps.

"Oh, I guess it was those Uncle Sam Needs You posters that made it seem unpatriotic for unmarried nurses not to join the reserve."

She told me about her brief basic training and what fun she and the other newly inducted nurses had had on their transport that had come in with the convoy. She talked about the hospital on Corregidor and how she really enjoyed military life, but she'd hardly had a chance to find out what the Nurse Corps was all about before the Japanese bombs had come screaming down.

"It all happened so fast. You can't believe how disorganized it was."

"Oh, can't I?" and we laughed about the blunders and crazy things we had each experienced through the month of December.

"And where were you when we needed help out there on Bataan?"

"Believe me, Doris, staying in Manila wasn't our idea. Harriet MacLean went out with the surgical team from Santa Scholastica, and the rest of us were left behind. Did you happen to run into her?"

"No, I sure didn't."

"I guess it was pretty rough out there."

"Yeah, I'd say so," Doris said lightly. "I was in Hospital #2 on Bataan. You would have died laughing if you'd seen our open-air nurses quarters. They were behind sheets draped over jungle brush." She joked about bathing in a nearby creek and about the sentries who kept soldiers from "mistakenly" wandering into their sanctum sanctorum.

She talked about the quiet days when things were slow, how she and some of the other nurses had gone swimming in the beautiful cove on the Mariveles coast. She described the Army's field hospitals with wards out under the trees, and she laughed about how the patients called them the

Angels of Bataan.

She jumped, laughing, from describing one thing to another, but after what the bedraggled civilian women had told us, somehow her stories didn't ring true. She said nothing about the rows and rows of beds and how each one had to be made into two by putting mattresses on the ground and covering the springs with boards and blankets or whatever else could serve the purpose. And still there had not been enough beds.

She failed to talk about the demanding and exhausting hardships or the dwindling medical supplies and the food shortages. No mention was made of patients with gangrenous limbs, patients who had to be placed away from the others because the stench was so awful. I heard nothing about the protective nets that kept the flies away while the decomposed tissue was eaten away by maggots.

Nothing was said about the bomb that hit Hospital #2 or the horror of seeing arms, legs, and other body parts hanging on tree branches; nothing about the terror-stricken eyes of soldiers afraid to let go of a nurse's hands; nothing about the agony of the dying. She did not tell me about all the dead, or about the helplessness she must have felt at being unable to do more for her patients.

She laughed about the trucks that came in the middle of the night, about the sergeant who didn't give them much time to pack a suitcase. But there was nothing about how heartbreaking it was to say good-bye. She made it sound so funny when she talked about the cussing truck driver trying to find his way in the dark and getting lost. She laughed about how they almost didn't make it, laughed about how emotionally drained she felt when she saw the *Canopus*'s tunnels going up in flames.

I marveled at how well Doris handled this, how she laughingly described the huge Malinta tunnel within the rock island with its laterals running out from a 275-foot main branch and the multidecked bunks used for patient beds. There was nothing about the continuous rumbling of exploding bombs, about the stinking and stifling dust-ladened air, or about how eerie and frightening it was when the generators went out during bombings. Neither did she mention the continuous line of incoming casualties, nor the many wounds she had cleaned and sutured, nor the exhausting strain of trying to keep patients alive.

But I could see Doris's lips begin to tremble. I wanted to say something helpful, but not knowing what to say, I said nothing.

After a deep breath she added, "Dottie, you should have seen Ma Crawford when the Japanese general made his inspection on the parade grounds! She stood as stiff as a ramrod between the other two senior nurses, and the rest of us were lined up behind her." She laughed. "He didn't seem to know what to do about us."

"Yes, I can imagine," I said, and, again noting her trembling lips, I changed the subject. "Well, tell me, did any of our other classmates join the services?" And then we talked and laughed about incidents in our nurses training and life in Santo Tomas.

"I see the chow line is beginning to form," she said after awhile, getting up to leave, but, teary-eyed, she sat down again. "Oh, God, Dottie, it was a living hell out there!"

"I'm sure it was," I said, and, with an arm over her shoulder, I cried along with her. She and the others had done so much. They were there during those long months when nurses were needed most, but what about me? Oh, Blessed Mary, Mother of God, pray for them and for me. Oh, merciful God, thank you for sparing me this, and forgive my cowardly thoughts.

Some internees did get to go out once in a while for camp business, but always with a guard escort. When the *Teia Maru* came in with tons of International Red Cross supplies, a work party was sent to Pier 7 to unload. Japanese imprinted postcards, issued to and then collected from us, went out on the ship to Tokyo, where they were censored before going farther. Knowing this, one couldn't say much in the twenty-five words we were allowed. "I am fine" (even if we weren't) and "I love and miss you" took up a third of the space, but at least relatives would know we were still alive on 1 November 1942.

Work parties from Bilibid also were sent to the pier, and when the guards weren't looking, a few words were exchanged. Thus we heard about the Navy corpsmen and patients who comprised the cast for a propaganda film made on Corregidor, showing enthusiastic basketball teams and an applauding audience.

"At least they said thanks and gave us each a pack of cigarettes," we heard.

We also learned that the Bilibid POWs knew "Wicked Major Siki," and that he liked to gloat over the films he showed them, films that had been taken from Japanese bombers during the attack on Pearl Harbor.

"See there?" he apparently said, "you have no navy!" Who did he think he was kidding?

But the Major's attempts to demoralize our men did not work. No one doubted that freedom was right around the corner. Three more months, then another three months, and so on until we were free. An attitude of self-pity and hopelessness could indeed hasten one's death, but Yankee humor is usually pretty hard to beat down, as survivors well knew.

Lieutenant Nogi, who had replaced Captain Kusomoto and was a better business administrator, had little patience with Dr. Stewart's repetitious pleas for more nourishing food and badly needed medicine, but a truckload of patent medicines did make it through Bilibid's gate. The small amount of iron in Lydia Pinkham's Pink Pills For Pale [female] People and in Carter's Little Liver Pills was helpful, no doubt, but not as much as the psychological effect of American-made products. Best of all was the large quantity of powdered charcoal, a godsend for many patients with intestinal problems.

There were no entrepreneurs in Bilibid. A canteen provided produce and specially ordered items now and then, but after the guards had helped themselves there wasn't much left.

Gonorrhea was a serious problem among the guards, and those infected with venereal diseases were severely punished before they were treated. Consequently they would gladly pay the corpsmen five pesos each for sulfathiazole tablets. With peso signs dangling in front of their eyes, the corpsmen made molds and combined chalk, kaolin, and sugar to create lookalike Winthrop's sulfathiazole tablets, complete with the familiar groove across the center.

Business went along very well until a dubious young Japanese officer wanted the tablets checked out by the Sternberg laboratory. To pass their inept tests, one of the doctors suggested adding a little sulfanilamide powder. Thus business continued to flourish as nicely as the customers' social diseases.

Thanksgiving came and went. One evening Miss Redecker came into our room and said solemnly, "Twenty-five pesos for each of us."

"Oh, how nice," Julia said. "And who do we thank for this?"

"If you do not ask, I will not have to answer," the chief nurse said, and that was that.

It wasn't much, but money meant replenishing the most basic of necessities. We hadn't seen a paymaster for over a year, and the two hundred pesos we'd each brought from Santa Scholastica was all but gone.

The military prisoners hadn't been paid either, not until now. Their captors certainly hadn't bent over backward to follow the Geneva Treaty concerning POWs, but when representatives from the International Red Cross visited, they may have wanted to look good. Whatever the reason, each prisoner was now to receive wages commensurate with those of the Japanese military.

From Navy captains and Army and Marine Corps colonels down to ensigns and second lieutenants, monthly pay ranged from 310 to 85 pesos. From this, 60 to 40 pesos were deducted for subsistence and a percentage of the balance was put into a compulsory savings in a Tokyo bank. This left 25 pesos in hand for the top officers and 6 pesos for the lowest-rated enlisted men.

"Our nurses are not being paid," Dr. Stewart had said, and Miss Redecker was too deeply touched by their sacrifice to share this information with anyone. It was a noble gesture that may have repeated itself had not their monthly cash on hand been reduced to 3 pesos. The rest was collected by the Japanese for unexpected expenses.

With Christmas in the offing, internees busied themselves making toys out of pieces of wood or whatever was available. Lively knitting needles and crochet hooks turned string and yarn into socks, shawls, sweaters, even dolls. Choirs practiced. Teenagers made paper decorations and planned parties. The arrival of the Red Cross supplies could not have come at a better time.

Everyone watched expectantly as trucks brought in cases upon cases, each marked as having been released from a Red Cross warehouse in South Africa and contributed by European Allies. There were large cans of meats and vegetables, dried fruit, dehydrated potatoes, bulk powdered soap, cigarettes, shampoo, shaving cream, clothing, shoes. So much, yet so little for so many.

Individual Comfort Kits created more excitement than all else. Each case contained four kits, and each kit, shared by two internees, was filled with small cans of meat, fish, and a fifteen-ounce can of powdered milk. There were little packets of butter, cheese, sugar, raisins, prunes, crackers, a candy bar, a bar of soap, and something we hadn't heard of before: a two-ounce jar of instant coffee. Right away items were bought, sold, or swapped, and some of us set aside cans of powdered milk for the children in the months ahead.

It promised to be a good Christmas. Kodaki and Kuroda realized the importance of religious holidays and did not object to the amazing volume of brightly wrapped presents that showed up in the Package Line.

For the haves, Christmas Day brought visitors

— friends and servants bearing the makings of mouthwatering feasts. Filipinos were allowed to spend a few hours with their interned American husbands and fathers. Even the weather cooperated.

Considering the circumstances, it was an exceptional day, one filled with brotherly love and hope. Prayers from the well-attended church services must have flooded the heavens, and I was confident that God smiled fondly on my prayers for Johnny, the *Houston*, and everyone else I could think of.

It was a special holiday, saddened by haunting memories of past Christmases spent with family and friends. Sad too were the heartbreaking and tearful good-byes after such short but joyous reunions of Filipino-American families.

Christmas in the POW camps also was brightened by the Red Cross supplies, we heard. Stirring church sermons and familiar Christmas carols and hymns had far deeper meanings than ever before for these men.

And then it was on to 1943, which would be "a year of glorious achievements," the *Manila Tribune* said. Yes indeed, we said, '43 and we'll be free!

14

OVERCROWDING

Pulling weeds and planting seeds in Cabanatuan's expansive gardens was anything but glorious or much of an achievement for the prisoners. They were required to work in an awkward straight-legged posture, and if they straightened up when a guard happened to be around, a healthy whack with a "vitamin stick" (rifle) across the middle of the back could do serious physical damage.

The most glorious achievement here was the thriving sales of the phony sulfathiazole tablets by corpsmen who'd been transferred from Bilibid. Chortling doctors wondered what postmortem findings might reveal on those who routinely took these plaster of paris tablets.

Glorious, too, were the work parties who repaired runways on Clark and Nielson airfields, where nothing was too good for the Emperor's Eagles. When the guards (who unknowingly had nicknames like Duckbutt, Cherry Blossom, White Angel, and Charlie Chaplin) weren't looking, extra sand went into the cement mixers. After that fine achievement, one of the POWs might get to watch Flying Dragon bombers standing on their noses or Zero fighters flipping over on their backs.

In Bilibid, glorious was Dr. Walters, who defied the odds by saving lives that would otherwise have been lost. A hard-nosed perfectionist, he would never have won a popularity contest, and he didn't care. Brisk and demanding, he got things done. Considering what he had to work with, no sterile linen, no caps and masks, no sterilizer, dressings soaked in creosote solutions, and only an overworked antiseptic solution for tired rag sponges and repeatedly used instruments, this was a remarkable achievement.

In Santo Tomas we achieved nothing so glorious, but we did deal with our problems and unique circumstances as best we could. Our committee of order had to confront issues such as pregnancy (in clear violation of the "no hugee, no kissee, no touchee, no babies" rule), gambling, and out-of-bounds violations. Weeping mothers-to-be were carted off to Holy Ghost College, and the Pregnant Father's Club members were jailed. There were threats to separate men from women altogether if they couldn't conduct themselves properly.

And then there were the misdeeds of John Geisner.

Stairwells leading to the classrooms on the roof were out of bounds, but Geisner immediately put his bed and belongings on a little-used landing above the third floor. He was told to move into one of the classrooms, but he defiantly refused.

No one on the committee on order wanted to turn over a countryman to the enemy, and the committee chose to ignore him. If the Japs caught him, that was his bad luck. He was ignored by Sackett's executive committee as well until incensed citizens brought his bed-renting activities to light.

"You touch my stuff and I'll give Kodaki an earful," he threatened.

"We'll talk to him ourselves if we must."

The sneering Geisner was moved, bed and bundle, and he stormed over to the commandant's office to announce that he was an enlisted man in the U.S. Army and could name several other servicemen in the camp.

"All military men are to report to the commandant's office immediately," came promptly over the PA system, and the camp was horrified.

"Costello," I said when I finally found him, "I can't begin to tell you how sorry I am."

"I'm sorry too, ma'am. But like Pa always says, there's bound to be a few rotten apples in the barrel."

A *Tribune*'s headline read JAPAN SET FOR NEW DRIVE IN NEW GUINEA. Along with some of the other off-duty nurses, I was lying on my bed on this dull afternoon looking at the cracks in the ceiling. Now that crack looks like it could be a staircase to the moon, but is it? Oh, dear God, how awful to have nothing better to do than this!

Depressed, I thought about Johnny and wondered why I had gotten involved with the idiot in the first place. Uh oh, Sarah's magazine is about to fall on her face. No, it isn't. It's slipping down onto her chest. Too bad Velda's lending library didn't work out. Mending books was something to do. Oh, yuk! I'm so sick of looking at dingy laundry hanging on our mosquito nets to dry.

Bobbie seems to be doing okay now. Uterine tumors and a hysterectomy. Recluse Amy is propped up against her pillow, as usual, with her notebook and pencil. Liz says she writes poetry.

Liz at least has a good sense of humor, but when she's facing the wall like that, she's in a bad mood. You'd think she'd learn after a session in the Philippine General with pleurisy, but who can account for some peoples' reasoning? So she doesn't like mongo beans, telinium tastes like spinach, and what does she say about taking cold showers in the chilly wee hours of the morning? "Shower in front of all those women? I'll die first!"

And Ellen. There she is, dreamily unraveling what she has just knitted. Reminds me of Penelope waiting for Ulysses to return from the Trojan War. Darn it, she's so sensitive, and Liz shouldn't pick on her the way she does. Nasty remarks can be downright hurtful.

And Olga. I swear she couldn't exist if she lost her hairbrush and mirror. You'd think she was getting ready to go out on a date.

Dammit, I'm so sick of these women!

And it wasn't only the nurses I'd had my fill of; there were too many people everywhere. People seemed to be coming out of the woodwork, not only in the Big House, but also in the Educational Building, the gymnasium, everywhere.

And, with the increasing number of tuberculosis patients, something had to be done. The former camp hospital could serve as an isolation unit if the Army nurses moved into the Big House. In two of the large classrooms, they would have more usable floor space, if not their enviable privacy. When it came to the bottom line, no alternative could be found.

"Can you blame them for not wanting to move?" somebody asked.

"They'll simply have to give a little, just like everybody else," came the retort.

And so on. Then, during a visit with Doris, I discovered that the Army nurses had decided to go out on strike over the matter.

"I think it's a terrible mistake," Doris said, "but that's what they're planning."

"Go out on a strike?" It was a whispered shout. "I've never heard of nurses going out on a strike. Oh my, Doris, you can't *do* that!"

"Well, they're not showing up for work tomorrow."

"How about the night shift?"

"It'll be covered tonight."

"That'll leave just us and the civilian nurses?"

"I guess so."

"Oh well, these things have a way of ironing themselves out."

"Yes, they do," Doris said optimistically. "See you later."

I found everyone sitting around the shanty table together, surprisingly, and asked what I had missed.

"Nothing other than poor Lizzy rapidly growing old." There was a partially eaten birthday cake in the center of the table.

"It's really good, even if it is made with cassava flour," Liz said, and the breezy conversation seemed to indicate that the next day was under control.

I waited for a lull and said, "Miss Redecker, am I to go on duty tomorrow?"

"My dear girl, you know that neither Julia nor I make out the schedule," she said.

"Well," I said, "I thought that since the Army nurses are going out on strike tomorrow, I would . . . have . . . been . . ."

"Miss Still! What are you saying?"

I knew that Doris would never speak to me again, but this was important. I related the facts as she'd told them to me.

And so, at seven o'clock the next morning, I sheepishly marched behind Miss Redecker and the other nurses assigned to the first shift as they resolutely went in the hospital's front door. The night nurse at the front desk smiled and gave the change of shift report as though nothing unusual was going on. Then another night nurse showed up. It was Doris!

Straight-faced, she went about her last-minute tasks, but I managed to corner her before she left.

"Doris, honestly I didn't mean to . . ."

"That's okay," she said amiably, "we were counting on you."

Well, damn you!

Strikebreaker animosity that could have developed was overshadowed by Mr. Kodaki's broadcast over the PA system. "Authorities in Japan have graciously granted permission to move this internment camp to Los Baños, a spacious location on an agricultural college campus where —"

"They can't *do* that."

"Shh! Be quiet and listen!"

"Will benefit not only you, but bring relief to your countrymen in the city for whom there is no room here. Los Baños is an ideal health resort, with its mineral baths. You will find the open country is —"

"What about the Package Line?"

"Doggone it, hush!"

"Husbandry will provide more meat. Vegetable gardens in this fertile land will . . ."

The way Kodaki pictured it, Los Baños was too good to be true, but despite his flowery words, it was no more inviting to us than Siberia would have been. His message was delivered on 9 May 1943, and he expected an initial group of eight hundred able-bodied men to be ready to leave on 14 May.

Volunteers were requested, but many of the two hundred and fifty who signed up recanted when it became known that they were to build living quarters for nearly ten thousand people.

Kuroda was upset. He wanted the complete list within the hour, which meant the committee had to pull names at random. Only so many unattached men were available, so those with wives in Santo Tomas but no children were singled out.

As an added inducement, Kodaki said married couples and families could live together when the barracks had been built and that marriages would be allowed. With this in mind, the prospect of going out the front gate took on a rosier hue.

On 12 May, Joyce came running up to me. "Geez, I've been looking all over for you!" she said breathlessly. "Miss Redecker wants us all to come over to the shanty right away!"

As usual, our chief nurse came right to the point. "Dr. Lloyd and Dr. White have asked us to go to Los Baños and help set up the hospital. How do you feel about this?"

For just a moment, thoughts of leaving familiar ruts and routines for the unknown left us at a loss for words, but when Miss Redecker reminded us time was wasting, we all said yes, we would like to go.

With that settled, the Marine Corps' magical spirit of Semper Fidelis filled Room 30A's back corner. No more sitting around moping. So much to do, so little time. We laughed and joked as we bumped into one another.

But when it was time to ship out our personal belongings on 13 May, it was frightening. Except for what we wore, the contents of our small handbags were all we were left with. Gone were the special jars, tin cans, extra bars of sparingly used soap, decks of bent cards, buckets, pots, pans, clothes, beds, everything.

Would we ever see them again?

Before dawn on 14 May, a bugler's reveille on the PA system awakened a festive air in the camp.

As departure time approached, the front yard was in a turmoil with sentimental handshaking, pats on the back, emotional moments for husbands and wives and engaged couples, last-minute words between those going and those staying.

Fascinated by the high-spirited excitement, the guards watched as the trucks filed out the front gate. More trucks, more hands waving, more V for Victory signs. A smiling guard who unintentionally responded in kind was thoroughly mortified.

We were among the last to leave, and wives came over to say, "Take good care of our men until we get there."

Several of the Army nurses came to wish us well, a pleasant sendoff that let us know we had been appreciated after all. "If the war ends before we get to Los Baños, I'll see you in the States," Doris said with a good-bye hug.

"Anchor's Aweigh" was played as we got onto

the truck, and equally unexpected was the heartfelt applause from internee friends we didn't know we had.

"I must be allergic to something," Miss Redecker said as she wiped her eyes and dabbed at her nose, and she wasn't the only allergic nurse on the truck.

Strings of freight trains stood at Tutuban railroad station, less than ten miles northwest of Santo Tomas. The long series of metal boxcars attached to the only steaming locomotive was obviously meant for us, and we watched as earlier arrivals boarded them. "Heavenly day!" Julia exclaimed. "They're closing the doors on the men in the boxcars!"

"Oh dear! They will suffocate!" Miss Redecker said. Equally concerned were the two doctors and Mr. Caldwell, the appointed chairman of the administration committee for Los Baños, and the Japanese lieutenant in charge agreed to open the doors on one side, letting the three men know that they would be held personally responsible if anyone tried to escape.

Two nurses were assigned to each of the first six cars.

"You girls sit here," insisted the men in the open space, and so Olga and I were to ride sitting with our feet hanging over the side.

At length there were a few short whistle blasts and the train jerked and rattled as it slowly made its way out of town. After twenty minutes or so, those in the back thought they were being cooked alive, and a rotation at given intervals was agreed upon.

"No, no. You girls stay where you are," the men said as the train kept chugging along ever so slowly, as though its cargo were too heavy.

Everyone settled down to quiet conversations. With my head propped against the metal opening, I was aware only of the monotonous dirgelike sound as the wheels rolled rhythmically over the ties.

I imagined the beautiful Tagaytay ridge right over there. What a view from its lodge. Lake Taal. A lake within an island within a lake within an island, or something like that. Four of us nurses and our dates had gone there in one of the Navy Yard's station wagons.

Johnny and his laughing eyes. A smoothie, and I'd fallen for him, hook, line and sinker. Of all the men I've dated, I thought, I could have married Pete Dalton, the man of the hour in nurses' training, and I would never have joined the Navy in the first place. It could have been Jerry, the aviation cadet on North Island. It could have been any number of nice guys, but no. Well, Johnny, you're not the only fish in the sea.

Poor Mom and Dad. They must be awfully worried, but what can I do other than pray for them?

15

LOS BAÑOS

The city of Los Baños was 70 kilometers south-east of Santo Tomas, at the lower end of Laguna de Bay, and the camp was four or five kilometers northeast as the crow flies. The men walked to it from the train station, and we nurses rode in the back of a sputtering coal-burning truck. From the top of a range, we looked down a northward-sloping valley into a bucolic setting under a beautiful sky. Wildflowers, chirping birds, clean, fresh air. The unique fragrance of chico blossoms mixed with barnyard odors.

The road led to the back gate's archway, in which a barbed-wire fence enclosed fifty-five acres of the University of the Philippines' extensive Agricultural College. In front of the gate, a short wooden bridge went over a gurgling stream. Inside the archway was a newly built guardhouse, and across the dead-end road, Roosevelt Road, as the internees would name it, lumber, sections of prebuilt nipa roofing, rolls of sawali, and other building materials were stacked. These belonged to a Japanese contractor who would build the barracks with the help of Filipino laborers — taos.

Apart from this fenced-off area, other building materials had been stacked. Bought with camp funds, these would be used to remodel, upgrade, and maintain the camp.

We passed a pink stucco infirmary that dominated the banks of the stream. On the other side of Roosevelt was what looked like a weed patch, possibly an overgrown garden. Among the many buildings were a gymnasium, a YMCA building, a chapel, dormitories, and cottages. There was a soccer field, a baseball diamond, and a bandstand, which would surely help to fend off boredom for internees. A barbed-wire fence surrounded the entire compound.

The eight hundred men were housed in the gym and the eight small cottages; the nurses in one of the dormitories. It was tight living quarters for the men, but the new camp's tranquillity was inspirational.

The U-shaped infirmary, overlooking a large courtyard, was a mess on the inside. Judging from the assortment of garbage within, it must have been used first by transient Philippine Scouts and American troops, then possibly by Japanese soldiers or foraging Filipinos. Except for a few battered pieces, all furnishings were gone. Some of the cupboards and shelves had been ripped off the walls, and dust-laden spider webs in the spacious rooms obviously hadn't been disturbed for some time.

The infirmary's front door opened into a waiting room surrounded by several doors and hallways. A hallway between the clinic and the surgery room led to a balcony that gave access to several wards, and from this balcony, one could also look down into a courtyard.

Wrought-iron stairs led down to storage rooms, a pharmacy, a kitchen, and a one-bedroom apartment that extended across the lower end of the building. The kitchen and apartment each had two outside doors, one that opened into the courtyard and one to an outside path.

Inside the surgery, rusty hinges on the built-in autoclave groaned painfully. A portable instrument sterilizer looked as though it had shorted out when someone had tried to cook rice in it. All that remained in the kitchen was its sink, and wiring in the gaping hole in the wall indicated that an electrical outlet had come out with a stove's plug.

Yes, it was a mess, but with so many available hands, we converted the infirmary into a hospital with remarkable speed. The Japanese brought in an assortment of surgical instruments and an operating table that must have been a museum piece. Dr. Bailey's dental chair and instruments from his Manila office were brought in, at his suggestion. Lab supplies and equipment came in from fellow internee Julius' downtown laboratory, and Bobbie groaned at the sight of an old-fashioned wood-burning stove that showed up.

Lizzy, who was to run the clinic, said she needed a "dressing cart" with this-and-that, and lo and behold, there it was just as she'd described it!

"Liz, where did Austin and his bearded shadow ever find the wheels?"

"I guess the commandant won't be riding his bicycle for a while."

The pharmacy began to look and smell like one, and the storeroom became pretty well organized. The clinic had customers right away, and now that the wards were ready, the hospital staff was increased by two janitors and eight orderlies who hadn't been in a hospital since they were born, if then. Bobbie's kitchen had breakfast, lunch, and supper "chefs" whose previous experience consisted of flipping steaks on a barbecue grill.

Shanties popped up farther down from the gymnasium, speakers were mounted in the bandstand, the recreational area was cleaned up, and out came the athletic equipment.

The weed patch was cleaned up, and seeds were planted in symmetrical lines. Cleaning the stagnant reservoir and repairing the water pump seemed to take forever.

Temporary water shortage was only one of the inconveniences, but life was beautiful here compared to Santo Tomas, and the dormitory was a welcome relief from Room 30A. When it wasn't raining, summer twilights were long and colorful. Frequently when we went for a walk or sat outside, some of the men would join us to chat, and soon we would all be visiting and laughing.

And there were new people to get to know right in our little hospital family. One day, engrossed in the list of supplies to be picked up downstairs, I nearly tripped over Loren Mitchell squatting outside the kitchen door with a dustpan in one hand and a brush in the other. He was a clean-shaven fellow with neatly combed dark hair except for a stubborn strand curling rakishly over his forehead. I didn't remember seeing him around before, but then a shave and haircut could make quite a difference.

I ran into him again that evening when some of us were sitting out on the lawn, and before long he came over to sit beside me. "The chief tells me you're a fellow Californian," he said. "What part of the state are you from?"

"Southern California. Long Beach when I was a little girl, but I lived in Burbank before I became a nurse."

"Well, I'll be dogged. My kid sister and I spent summers in Long Beach with our grandparents. Hollywood Hills was home while I attended Cal Tech in Pasadena."

We talked about how we had both visited the Griffith Park Observatory in Hollywood Hills, Grauman's Chinese Theatre, and the Palladium Ballroom. We decided we must have splashed around in the Los Angeles Bimini pool at the same time, and we and our siblings had probably destroyed one another's sand castles at Long Beach.

"Well, tell me," I said, "have you lived in the

Philippines long?"

"Live here? No. I flew Lockheed PBYs out for the Dutch. We came in three flights of nine planes, and this was my third trip out."

He said the pilots and navigators were ordinarily flown home commercially from these trips, and the rest of the crew would go back on a ship. But in December 1941, they were booked on the *China Clipper*'s last flight out when they were bumped by a couple of Japanese officials.

"The other pilots and navigators chose to go out on a ship, but Charlie over there, who was in charge of ground operations, thought he could arrange a flight to Australia on a military plane for the navigator and me."

"And you didn't make it."

"It's the chance you take. We wanted to be home for Christmas."

"Where was home when you came out here?"

"Coronado was where my wife and sons were when I left, but I imagine they've moved closer to her parents by now. I have a son who was one month old when I left."

Over the loudspeakers, Brahms' "Lullaby" said it was curfew time.

I frequently ran into Mitch at the hospital, and more often than not I found myself in his company in the evenings as cliques developed. He was such a gentleman, but I was amazed at how rudely Charlie talked to him, at first. Then I realized they were just pals teasing each other.

Charlie was a sharp-minded fellow with a sense of humor.

Both Mitch and Charlie were concerned about the camp's future. The reservoir was too small, and the twenty-five-bed hospital would not be big enough to service a population larger than the eight hundred we already had. Barracks were being built, each thirty by ninety feet. Built to accommodate ninety-six internees, two of them were to have cubicles for married couples. But would there be enough room for everyone?

Space problems aside, there were construction foul-ups. Sidewalk superintendents thought the frameworks wouldn't support the soaked thatch roofs in a storm, and the Filipino laborers' solution to this was to put the roofs up again after the storm.

The barbed-wire fence around the construction site was meant to prevent communication between the internees and the Filipino workers and to protect supplies from sticky internee fingers. It didn't work. Midnight raiders built shelves for themselves in the gymnasium and other such conveniences, and eventually Mr. Caldwell, head of the administration committee, was called to the commandant's office where Earl, Mitch's navigator, was being detained.

"This man steal Japanese property," the interpreter said. "Lieutenant Colonel Narusawa say you give him good punishment right away."

And so the discipline committee had to decide what to do. Gerrad, Earl, and Mr. Caldwell came looking for Mitch and Charlie.

"Can't deny it," Earl said. "I was caught red-handed."

"Sentencing him is not my responsibility," Gerrad said. "It's been settling minor disputes so far, but where do we go from here when an arrest is warranted?"

"Let Mitch be the judge," Charlie snorted. "He's such a righteous ass."

"Do you mind, Mitch?" Caldwell said. "Let's get this over with."

And so it was. Mitch was the chairman of the board of judges, without a board, at least for now.

With this settled, Caldwell relaxed and talked about how both Kodaki and Kuroda had been down here a few times, and yes, he had pointed out the camp's shortcomings. Caldwell had spent a few days in Santo Tomas and reported that it looked like an old folks' home now. So many disabled and elderly people had been brought in that it had created a real problem for the camp's work force who had to take care of them.

Then Caldwell asked Mitch to come up with a sentence right away, and Mitch said he and Earl had already decided on one.

"Good grief," I said when Mitch told me about it, "that's a pretty stiff sentence for stealing a few nails."

"We had to satisfy the Japs."

"Ten days in that filthy outhouse?"

"That's Earl's idea. He's washing it down himself and he'll put lime in the pit and cover it with dirt. I still think ten days is longer than necessary, but that's what he thought it should be."

Earl didn't mind. He was not confined to just the outhouse, but to a grassy area where he could socialize with his friends over the flimsy fence.

Ten days passed quickly, and soon he was standing in the chow line again and was back at work.

June was ending; half of 1943 was gone. The hospital had settled down under Miss Redecker's management. Julia made dressings and bandages out of our white uniforms or anything else that was usable. Since our custom-made uniforms were getting pretty shabby, she talked about doing something with the dungarees we had in our trunks.

Sarah puttered around in the surgery, sterilizing supplies as needed, and Bobbie kept busy in the galley. Liz, although she more or less ran the clinic, rotated along with the rest of us, especially on the afternoon and night shifts, and cases that couldn't be handled here were sent back to Santo Tomas. The workload was light, and admissions to our little hospital were mostly for dengue fever cases, recurrent malaria episodes, and other short-term but dramatic maladies.

The dormitory had distinct advantages over Room 30A, especially after Liz said, "How nice it would be if . . ." Builder Austin and his friend promptly leveled a section under the building, laid a wooden floor, built cupboards, and did everything else she had mentioned. It was supposed to be for all of us, but just as the shanty had really been Miss Redecker's, this was Lizzy's domain.

We didn't miss Room 30A one little bit, but some of the services in Santo Tomas were clearly lacking here. The one barber cut only men's hair, and so when Lizzy fretted about needing a haircut, I offered.

"Come on, Dottie," she said, towel, comb, and mirror in hand, and after a few mistakes, even Julia and Sarah took chances with their boyish bobs. I didn't mind. After all, this was my part in the group's strengthened give-and-take camaraderie.

The summer's rainy season brought slippery mud and accidents for the bakia-wearing internees. The clinic's caseload and ward admissions increased, and to most of the nurses, the inept orderlies were more trouble than they were worth.

"What do you expect? They're not corpsmen. Instead of bitching, why don't one of you give them a few lessons on simple nursing procedures?"

"Good idea, Dottie. I'll look around in my luggage. I might have something you can use."

"Wait a minute! It's you girls who are complaining, not me."

"It's your idea."

"And I give it to you. No strings attached."

In the meantime, Charlie and his co-workers

were critical of the way Barracks 1 and 2 were being built. Cement flooring was laid, but, "Ah, so sorry. No more cement."

In an "H" configuration, each two barracks were to be connected by a passage in which conventional sinks, toilets, and showers were to be installed, but rather than allow the Filipinos to make a mess of it, Charlie's gang volunteered to build the cesspools. Two were well under way when, "Ah, so sorry. No sinks, no toilets available."

"For Christ's sake!" said Charlie. "If they want to build outhouses, they'd better build 'em away from the barracks."

Next came a typhoon that uprooted trees and ripped off branches. Down went the two barracks, washing away a part of the camp's garden and flooding the main kitchen, but the heroic internees eagerly responded to the crisis with acetylene lamps.

I was on the night shift, with acutely ill patients to take care of.

"I wish I could be more helpful," orderly Mike said, not knowing how to cope with all the drama.

"It's okay. You're doing fine," I said, scurrying back and forth among the patients, pointing out little things that he could do successfully.

Velda was a patient again, and I spent a good part of the night with her. Now that the sulfanilamide drugs had lowered her temperature, I tried to make her more comfortable as I straightened her bed covers.

With the crack of dawn, after carefully going over early morning care with Mike and demonstrating wherever possible, I went down to the kitchen to wash the used medicine glasses.

"My goodness, it must be a mess out there," I said when Mitch came on duty.

"Guess you know the barracks collapsed."

Just then, Mike came down in a frenzy. "Ma'am! Harold is shivering something fierce, and I don't know what to do!"

I hadn't intended to be a teacher, but the orderlies were finding little satisfaction in what they were doing. "I like working in the hospital," Mike said, "but when I'm asked to do something for a patient, it'd sure help if I knew why and how I'm to do it."

His "why" gave me pause. They should know why. On the other hand, too little knowledge can be worse than none at all. How far should they be allowed to go? Helping corpsmen put into practice what they are taught in the Hospital Corps school is one thing, but teaching someone with no technical background whatever is another story. Can I successfully hold classes for them? I don't know the first thing about teaching. Mitch probably doesn't either, but he taught classes in Santo Tomas.

At suppertime he was farther back in the chow line, and I waited for him. "Mitch, I would like to do a little mind-picking," I said as we walked down Roosevelt Road.

"Pick away."

"Well, I'm thinking about —" and, stumbling over something in the road, I dropped my banana and lost half my tea.

"I swear, you and my kid sister are two of a kind. You both need caretakers. Come down to the shanty, and we can talk while we eat."

Once there, I went out to look at the stream, which had widened into a river here. Its rapid flow amazed me, as did the old footbridge that dangled precariously over it.

"Noisy, isn't it?" Mitch said loudly.

"I should say so. It's pretty here," I said, looking at the neglected chico grove on the other side. "What a nice place this sloping ground behind your shanty would be for a flower garden."

"Be our guest. Joe and I will turn the ground over and you can plant it."

"Thanks, but I'm afraid I don't have a green thumb."

"You said you wanted to do a little mind-picking. What do you have in mind?"

"I'm thinking about teaching a class, but I don't know how to go about it."

"Well, doll, you start from A and go to Z."

"Oh, Mitch! Be serious. I'm considering teaching basic nursing procedures to our orderlies. Very basic."

"All I can tell you is, first, know what you want to teach. Second, take it step by step, and third, keep it simple and in language they can understand. You'll give them hands-on instruction along the line, won't you?"

It didn't sound too difficult, and with Miss Redecker's agreement I set about preparing classes. Joyce had borrowed a copy of *Handbook of the Hospital Corps* to study before the war, and it was in her trunk. The other nurses offered to help, and equally encouraging, the orderlies took heart at the prospect of attending my classes. I surely didn't want to let them down, not that I could expect them to be corpsmen, and the handbook was a godsend.

Know what you want to teach. Take it step by step. Keep it simple and in language they understand.

"How's it going?" Mitch asked a few days later, when he saw me sitting outside studying the corpsmen's text. "I can see it now. There's the right way, the wrong way, and the Navy way. What are you reading that's tickling your funny bone?"

"Here it says, 'Extravagant habits are easily acquired when large amounts of supplies are around.' What a nice problem that would be for a change."

"That's something both the Army and Navy Medical Corps should take seriously. Military waste is phenomenal."

"Were you in the service?"

"Couldn't find a decent job after Cal Tech, so I became an Army Air Corps cadet. But I didn't like kowtowing and bootlicking, and I dropped

197

out after graduation."

"What kind of map is that?"

"It's a map of the heavens," and he put it into my outstretched hand. "I'm being pushed into giving a class on celestial navigation."

"That should be interesting. The North Star is something used in navigating, isn't it? I've often wondered which one it is."

"It's called Polaris. Here it is," he said, pointing it out on the map. "One of these clear evenings, I'll point it out to you."

16

SOMEONE SPECIAL

It was mid-July 1943. The colorful twilight had faded, and away from the streetlights, the stars stood out brightly enough for Mitch to keep his promise. From the darkest spot on the lawn, he pointed to the Little Dipper. "It's also known as Ursa Minor, and Polaris is the last star on its handle. It's the North Star, or the pole star, and it's about one degree away from the actual North Pole. Over there is Ursa Major . . ."

"The Big Dipper."

"Right. The Big Dipper, with its pointer stars. An extended imaginary line drawn through the two stars at the lower end of the pan will come within five degrees of Polaris."

For the rest of the evening, he talked about the fascinating mysteries of the universe. He talked about the twelve constellations of the zodiac that were identified and named by astronomers two thousand years ago. He talked about dead-reckoning navigation practiced by the ancient mariners, about compasses and the north and south magnetic fields. He explained at length the characteristics of the wandering planets, saying that

Mars and Jupiter were getting visibly closer to one another and his students were making bets on when they would pass one another.

It was an interesting but confusing short course in astronomy that ended with Brahms' "Lullaby," again.

"Mitch, what's that bright star over there?"

"Oh golly, I don't know, but I'll give it to you."

"You don't mean it! A star of my very own?"

"It's all yours. Name it to suit yourself."

In bed, it wasn't easy to keep my mind on the rosary. In fact, I had to repeat a few decades because I was laughing to myself. I had heard lots of original lines in the Navy, I had received some rather unusual gifts, but no one had ever given me a star.

"Girls," Julia said, "now that we have the time to do it, let's rip the dungarees apart. We'll make uniforms out of them using what we're wearing as patterns. I'll cut them out, you baste them, and I'll sew them. I'll make the buttonholes, but it will be up to you to sew the buttons on and put the hems in."

This was something we really needed. Going through our trunks and footlockers was a nostalgic trip that could bring more tears than smiles if one were not careful. Dungarees retrieved, we each hoped to find an overlooked garment that could be washed, but all that were left were the Dry Clean Only's.

Looking through my trunk was also an opportunity to look for something nice to wear to my class. What the heck, I thought. Might as well look like a civilized human being while I'm teaching the orderlies. And it would be nice to wash with real soap.

Stateside soap was a memory. One could make it if one had the right ingredients: lye leached from wood ashes, coconut oil, and borax, if available. Charlie had experimented with it in Santo Tomas, he said, and when he'd tried it out on his shirt, all that was left were the buttons.

Trial and error had brought improvements, not that it could be used very successfully in hand-washing this old street dress. But I would try. Even if the material shrunk and its colors ran into one another, Julia could use it for something. Maybe armslings?

And so, on the appointed evening, in my pressed dress, my hair freshly washed and dabs from what little makeup I had left, I confidently hummed a cheerful tune on my way to teach my students in the bodega. After I set out what I was going to use in demonstrations, I noticed there were more in attendance than expected. "This is a class for the hospital orderlies," I said, and the extra men explained that they were considering applying for an orderly job when more people came down from Santo Tomas.

Before long, looking into a sea of dreamy faces, I realized that they weren't paying attention to what I was saying. Then it dawned on me. It's the way I'm dressed! Who am I reminding them of? Their faraway sweethearts? Their wives back home? Their dream girls?

"Gentlemen, please don't go away," I said. "I have an errand to run quickly, but I'll be right back!" When I came back dressed as usual, the class soon dwindled to attentive orderlies.

In the weeks that followed, I had reason to be proud of my students. Joyce volunteered to teach them proper methods of collecting specimens for the lab, and she and others helped with the hands-on teaching. But if anything went wrong, it was my fault. Constructive criticism was always welcome, but at times it could be more destructive than constructive.

"Dorothy, you apparently didn't teach them the difference between iodine and gentian violet. One of your stupid corpsmen painted scabies with iodine, and the patient got an iodine burn."

"Olga, they are *not* corpsmen. They are orderlies. They are not my corpsmen, and furthermore, *they are not stupid!*"

"Honestly," she quietly said in disgust. "It was your idea to teach them."

"And who of you girls complained the loudest to begin with?"

"As long as you are teaching them, you should —"

"Oh, stick it in your ear!"

"Miss Still!" Miss Redecker exclaimed from her dormitory door. "Must I remind you that you are in the Navy Nurse Corps? Your conduct is very unladylike."

"Yes, ma'am," I answered petulantly, but my differences with Olga were not over.

A few days later, Olga had more to say. "One of your *orderlies* allowed a dysentery patient to eat a ripe papaya, as if he didn't have trouble enough. Another one of your *orderlies* apparently doesn't know how to monitor a Murphy drip, and . . . ."

I gritted my teeth and coldly said, "Why don't you make them *your* orderlies and teach them yourself?"

"You don't have to be so touchy. I was only —"

Miss Redecker rushed up the stairs and whispered, "Ladies! Ladies! What is this all about?"

"Oh, nothing," I said, glaring at Olga who merely shrugged her shoulders.

"Hereafter, keep your disagreements away from the patient rooms. Miss Still, I am ashamed of you."

"Yes, ma'am," I said, leaving to make my final rounds and thinking, You're always ashamed of me, you old bat! I'd like to see how you would handle this if you were in my position!

"Golly, I'm sorry," Chuck said, "I know a Murphy drip is supposed to be given drop by drop, but gee whiz. . . ."

"It's okay, Chuck. You couldn't help it when the rusty old clamp fell apart. That could have happened to anyone. You did the best you could, and no one can ask for anything more. I'm sure neither you nor the other fellows know how much we all appreciate the progress you've made, even if we don't always say so."

"You really think so?" he said, following me into the ward.

"If I only had my little handwritten probie notebook from nurses training, I could give you more comprehensive lessons."

"You've already taught us quite a bit," he said. And considering how the patients reacted to them, I guess I had at that.

Only one of the four occupants of the ward was acutely ill. His temperature fluctuated between 100 and 103 degrees, and every bone in his body ached. Even the movement of his eyeballs hurt.

"Oh, I feel like I'm gonna' die."

"Come on now. Nobody dies from dengue fever." I wiped his face with the damp cloth, rinsed it out, and put it over his eyes. "I know how miserable you must feel, and I'll ask Miss Sturges to give you something for that."

Patients on the other side of the room obviously had overheard what had happened at the front desk, because one of them joked, "If I didn't know better, I'd say someone had blown her top."

"Chuck, did you hear a ruckus going on?" I asked, wearing my usual happy face.

"Was there a ruckus?"

It was one thing to make light of an unpleasant situation in front of the patients, but it didn't quell my angry feelings. I gave the ward report to Olga as calmly as I could, but when she referred to my behavior as juvenile, it was all I could do to keep from hitting her. Gritting my teeth, I marched resolutely out the front door and stormed down Roosevelt Road.

"Mind if I walk with you?" Mitch said, falling in step with me.

I grunted something.

"Slow down, doll," he said, taking my arm, as I angrily imagined Miss Redecker writing this on my service record. After a while he added, "Want to talk about it?" and I vehemently let loose my frustrations.

Mitch didn't chide me for overreacting, nor did he sympathize with my hurt feelings. In fact, he made no comment whatever as he listened until I had said it all. "Now do you feel better?"

I smiled shakily and wondered why I had become so angry over something that I would ordinarily have handled differently.

August brought the noisy shuttle bus with some welcome news. First, instead of the originally proposed ten thousand internees from Santo Tomas and Manila, Los Baños was to have a maximum of three thousand, and the parent camp would remain the same. Second, we were issued some more Japanese postcards, and best of all, another repatriation was coming up for one hundred fifty internees, including fifteen from Los Baños. But we had to wait until the driver's next trip before learning the names of the lucky fifteen.

Doctors Lloyd and White, associated with the Rockefeller Institute, made the list. Why were some of the others listed and others not? Political pull? Where was the list made, and on what basis?

"Don't ask me," a former patient said, "but darned if I'm going to turn it down."

"The Chrysler Corporation must have a lot of clout."

"Heck, I'm not that big a wheel."

"Oh, aren't you the funny one!"

"If you girls give me the names and addresses of your relatives, I'll write to them as soon as I get there. And don't worry Miss Redecker, I'll put the list under the lining in my shoe, and I'll eat it if I have to." But he wouldn't have to eat it.

With the two doctors gone, only the dentist and Dr. Jolanski, head of the sanitation committee, remained. "I'll sign prescription requests if that'll help," Dr. Bailey said, "but until another M.D. comes in, you nurses and Allen will have to do the best you can." And Dr. Jolanski, with his doctorate in chemical research, was no help. He chided me, "If I had any art supplies here, I'd make a caricature of you. You with the turned-up nose."

"Oh really? I bought an art book and charcoal pencils, but it didn't take me long to find out I'm no artist. They're in my trunk, and you are welcome to them."

By this time most of the nurses had found common interests with people outside our own circle, and our relationships with one another improved considerably.

I spent more time at the shanty, with or without Mitch. I had been coerced into planting a garden by Joe, who had turned the ground over and supplied the seeds. I didn't know one seed from another, not that it mattered, nor did it matter if they grew. Working with the rich soil was rewarding enough. Best of all, because of its corner position along the top of the riverbank, it was a welcome retreat where I found solitude among the shrubs and plants, listening to the birds and the river.

The shanty itself was so sturdily built that it could take quite a beating from the storms. Rainwater drained from the thatch roof's overhang into a shallow ditch and kept the elevated dirt floor dry. It had been designed by men, for men. A little charcoal stove sat on a counter, and a blackened three-pound coffee can served as a coffee pot. A crude table and chairs took up much of the floor space, and a collection of cans (also known as pots and pans) and eating utensils sat on shelves.

Joe was seldom there, and the shanty was mostly frequented by Mitch's friends and those who came to see the "judge."

One day while I was there, Charlie came to see him. "There you are, you overeducated bore," he said, tossing his notebook onto the table and rolling a cigarette. "Want to show you somethin', professor."

"Good Lord," Mitch said, looking at the drawings, "what kind of monstrosity is this?"

"Who gives a damn what kind of monstrosity it is? Tell me what you think. Will it work?"

Now that the ten flattened barracks had been put back up again, the Japanese insisted on keeping the toilet facilities as planned. As an alternative to the outhouse concept, Charlie's idea was to use the old-fashioned hole-in-the-board version. But he would mount the board over a long tilted metal trough that would be flushed and would drain into the closed cesspools.

"Beats an open ditch," Mitch said, "but flushing it is going to be a bugaboo."

"Damn it, will you let me finish? Water's going to be piped into the bathrooms, ya jackass."

"Aw, come on, Charlie. With that little reservoir, you can't get a strong enough flow."

"I know! I know!" Charlie yelled impatiently, turning to the next page. "See this? It'll be a fifteen-gallon tank that'll be mounted several feet above the highest end of the trough. And see this?" He pointed to a drawing on the next page, one of a float fashioned after those in conventional toilet tanks. The difference was that when enough water had accumulated, the float would trip a lever and the whole tank of water would come gushing down through a large pipe and into the trough. "And thar she blows!"

"Holy Moses, you'd better not be sitting over one of those holes when the thing lets loose!"

"Well, at least you'd get your goddamn ass washed off."

"Charlie! Watch what you're saying!"

"Well, what do you think, teach?"

"Looks good."

"Charlie," I said, "does the trough have to be that close to the board?"

Although he looked at me acidly at the time, when these primitive ideas were finally executed, the women didn't have to worry too much about an unexpected external douche.

September 1943, and my vegetable garden flourished. It was more of a hobby than a necessity, because the camp's gardens grew with gusto. Besides that, the canteen sold fresh fruits and vegetables, raw sugar, and duck eggs, as well as smelly cheroots and low-grade tobacco by the kilo.

No one here went hungry. Breakfast included a large ladle of cornmeal mush, coconut milk, a spoon of raw sugar, and coffee. Lunch was mongo beans flavored with beef (carabao), and supper was vegetable stew with visible meat, a good serving of rice, usually a banana, and a cup of tea.

I don't exactly know how so much information slipped into the camp, possibly through the grapevine or the amazing Filipino bamboo telegraph, but we heard that the Japanese-backed Republic of the Philippines had become a reality and that the islands were to become independent in 1944, two years earlier than the American timetable. We also heard that the Filipinos knew their idol MacArthur would be back, and everything would be all right once again. As far as we were concerned, of course it would be.

In the meantime, my garden was doing so well that I had green onions, garlic, telinium, Swiss chard, and New Zealand spinach to share with Joe, Mitch, the nurses, and the hospital staff. The shanty had begun slightly to show my influence, I spent so much time there.

"Sometimes I think Joe would use it more frequently if I weren't here all the time," I said to Mitch one day.

"Don't worry, doll. As far as he goes, it's okay."

I was still uncomfortable about this, and after we picked up our mongo beans from the main kitchen, I suggested taking advantage of the picnic table under the dormitory.

"You go ahead if you like."

"Lizzy's on duty. She won't mind."

"Maybe so, but for me to do so would imply approval, and I can't do that."

"Approval of what?"

"Look at it this way, doll. When I make judgments against men for far less violations, I can't condone that."

"Condone what?"

"If Austin is caught stealing from the Japs, that's his hard luck. The fact is, the Jap contractor knows what's been stolen, and he takes it back from the camp's stockpile. No matter how noble Austin's intent, he gets a lot of satisfaction out of doing this, and it's wrong."

"He's not doing it for himself, he's . . ." Walking on, I didn't know what to say. For all I knew, the folding chairs made for us nurses could have been made indirectly from camp property. Was Lizzy aware of this? Probably not. Not a good Catholic like her.

"There's no point in saying anything about it, but as much as I admire Austin, I can't conscientiously be a part of it, directly or indirectly. Do you understand what I'm saying?"

"I guess so."

In the second week of September, the shuttle bus arrived with more passengers than usual. Italy's Fascist Grand Council had surrendered to the Allies, and the Italian civilians on Luzon had been rounded up and brought here. Most welcome was a doctor, and, for the Catholics, a priest.

"I am Kendell Foster," the doctor said, introducing himself at the hospital, and despite his amiable and boyish grin, no one doubted who would be in charge of the hospital. Baseball bat in hand, he would become a star player on softball teams; ax in hand, he would be one of the best wood-choppers. The hospital's apartment was soon cleared out for him and his many boxes of personal belongings.

"Lucille, he brought enough instruments to do major surgeries."

"That, dear Sarah, is what he intends to do."

Father John was not nearly so aggressive nor handsome, but he unobtrusively went out of his way to shake hands with everyone in camp. He had a rugged look about him and sure enough, we would discover that he liked to swing a hammer, dig ditches, tend the camp gardens, and pitch a mean ball. Father John was content to bunk in the gymnasium.

It was a pleasure to have them join in our evening discussions; each had so much to contribute. Father John had a stock answer to any questions about Catholicism, though: "If you're interested, sit in on the talks I'll be giving from time to time."

It was good to have a priest in camp, even though in confession, I slightly whitewashed the blow-up with Olga. He didn't question me, though, and a few days later Olga asked me to cut her hair as though nothing had happened.

When I wasn't working in my garden or preparing lessons during off-duty time, I tried to digest some of the technical books I'd found in the shanty. Sometimes Mitch read them to me. I'd always thought that if something was in print, it had to be correct. Mitch did not agree and would tear things apart, analyzing them. I became acutely aware of the power of print, a concept that had never occurred to me.

And he liked to point out grammatical errors in what he read. "Language changes with time," he would say. "Incorrectly spoken language can usually be understood, but unless basic principles are adhered to, written English can be misleading."

We also read fiction, and even a book Father

John loaned to Mitch. "You may find this interesting, Mitch," he said. "It's a collection of Cardinal John Henry Newman's nineteenth-century letters. Read *Apologia pro Vita Sua*. It's his answer to the Anglican criticism of his conversion to the Catholic faith. He was a top Anglican priest, a professor of theology at Oxford, and at age forty-five he converted into the Catholic faith. Dottie, you too might find it interesting."

Like Mitch, I had only a superficial knowledge of the fundamentals of either religion, which made it hard to relate to what was written. In his wordy style, the cardinal rambled on and on about who'd said what, and there were so many rationalizations that I was soon thoroughly lost.

"Mitch, read it to yourself, then tell me what it's all about."

When he was finished, he said, "His perfect English makes it a pleasure to read. If I were to become involved with a church, I would have to agree with him and become a Catholic."

"Would you really?"

"Except for the fact that I fall into an honest agnostic category. I can't truthfully believe that I have a soul or that there is a God."

But "God is a just God," Father John had said, "and as such, He cannot help but recognize the sincerity of the faithful, no matter what religion they adhere to." Then he added with a chuckle, "No matter how wrong they may be."

We returned the book to Father John, and following mass one morning, he asked me if I'd got anything out of it. I had to admit that without Mitch's help, it would have taken me forever to understand the Cardinal's rambling essay.

"By the way, Dottie, you know that Mitch is married."

"Of course I do, Father."

"We have several fine Catholic bachelors in camp."

"Thanks for worrying about me, but that's not necessary. Mitch is good company. He's like the big brother I never had, and that's where it ends."

"I wouldn't like to see you get hurt."

17

"COUNTRY CLUB" LIVING

No special services were held on Memorial Day in Los Baños, but it was different in Bilibid, where a POW commander led the officers and men on a march to the cemetery.

"Attention!" a Marine officer shouted, and they stood in a rigid salute while Lieutenant Nogi, Lieutenant Urabe, and Major General Sikiguchi took their places in a ceremony for the dead.

Two U.S. Army chaplains conducted the services. A prelude to "One Sweetly Solemn Thought" was followed by a moment of silence, after which there was a roll call of those buried there. "My Buddy" was played, and the Japanese placed a wreath of flowers. Finally, "Tenting Tonight" was played softly in the background while the senior chaplain said a prayer. The official Japanese party left after taps, and the assembly was dismissed. It was a solemn, dignified, respectful event, one that undoubtedly few of the scattered three hundred POW camps in the Far East were privileged to conduct.

In Los Baños, life went merrily on. On the PA

system in the evenings, the man playing the recordings interjected music from a radio he was listening to. Off-duty nurses would be dancing around on a beautiful evening to the rhythm of Guy Lombardo's "It's Only a Paper Moon" or Glenn Miller's "My Blue Heaven," when in might slip Jimmy Dorsey's "Tangerine." But of course, Brahms' "Lullaby" would soon spoil the whole thing.

We put on plays and organized other entertainment events. Lizzy was to play the lead character in *The Philadelphia Story*, a proposed radio show codirected by a Canadian and two Englishmen, and the cast spent hours rehearsing.

Some of us even made money. Charlie and the men who worked on the barracks billed the Japanese contractor 3,000 pesos for their labor.

"He accepted it?"

"Yeah, and he handed us an itemized bill for the coffee and sandwiches he gave us, not to mention missing hammers, saws, shovels, and everything else he could think of."

Much fun and laughter. One didn't have far to go to find it, but to be alone with one's thoughts was just as important. The garden was my place for this, a spot where I could find mental relaxation while running my fingers through the dirt and pulling weeds.

One day, the current commandant, Lieutenant Colonel Kimura, was also finding solace in the sight and sound of the river as he wandered along this side of the barbed-wire fence. Eventually the elderly officer, with the aid of his cane, made his way up the slope, but had Mitch not shown up, he probably would not have stopped.

He bowed politely and said something and, not because we were required to, both Mitch and I bowed in return. In Oxford English, he began to talk about the garden as he plucked leaves from the plants, crushed and smelled them approvingly, and told us how to protect them from the rain and sun. He obviously had respect for nature's ability to produce, and from the way he described it, he must have had beautiful flower gardens in his country estate in Japan.

"The war will be over soon, then you, too, can go home." He bowed again and walked on.

"Jap or not, there goes a gentleman," Mitch said. Then, with a sigh he added, "I might as well move that cupboard."

"It was only a suggestion."

"The things I put up with are enough to make a grown man cry. If it isn't your boss or the chief, it's one of you nurses. 'Do this.' 'Fix that.' 'Don't put it here, put it there.' Women. Who can understand their logic?"

"Cheer up, friend. I'll give you a chit for the chaplain, and you can have one hour of sympathy free."

"Oh, yeah?" He grabbed me threateningly. Still holding my arms, his grip relaxed, the laughter in his eyes died away, and for a moment we looked at each other solemnly. "You're a smarty miss, aren't you?" he said and gently pushed me away. We both went back to the tasks at hand.

Pleasant days like these outnumbered depressing ones. Hours were spent sharing books he would read out loud while I knitted string socks. Sometimes he would ramble on about various thoughtful and interesting subjects, so patient in answering my many questions. What a comfortable man to be around, I thought.

The noisy coal-burning shuttle bus always brought welcome news, if only rumors or worn copies of the *Manila Tribune*. We saw pictures and reports about the spectacular celebration for the newly formed Philippine Republic. There were parades and marching bands, impressive military flyovers, rockets bursting in the night sky.

The driver, Coop, also brought messages from the parent camp. The Christmas committee asked Los Baños to send two hundred Christmas gifts for the children; the medical committee said there weren't enough dentists in Santo Tomas and wanted Dr. Bailey sent back; several extra women and a few men asked to be included on the second transfer to Los Baños. As for politics, "I don't know much about that except you here in Los Baños don't know how lucky you are."

But we did; at least we thought we did.

We had our aggravations, but we knew they were minor. For instance, although Dr. Foster was popular, when he admitted a Japanese officer to the hospital's private room it was no more acceptable to us than the way he consistently overrode the administration committee by going directly to the commandant with his requests. Bobbie and her kitchen crew were especially annoyed with him when he had Julius move into the apartment with him. The flunky took it upon himself to store the doctor's canteen purchases in the refrigerator, and then he started cooking for him. Bobbie threatened to throw his simmering stew pot over the fence if he didn't stop using the hospital stove.

On the plus side, the doctor was a pretty handy fellow to have around when we nurses were sick. He diagnosed the annoying lump in my right groin as an inguinal hernia, and Miss Redecker supported his contention that it should be corrected before it got worse.

It turned out to be a hydrocele, rare in women. As long as he had gone this far, he decided to take my appendix out through the same incision, only to find that it had been about to rupture. True, I had been a little nauseated that morning, but I'd thought it was just nerves, and Julius's lab tests hadn't indicated an infection.

I was to remain in one of the two-bed wards for the customary twenty-one days following a herniotomy, and before long I had a roommate. Liz was admitted with a dengue-fever diagnosis, her temperature going sky high, and she rambled on about one thing or another. "Dear God, I'm dyin'. Don't want to be buried here. Want to be buried in the family plot back home."

"Lizzy, you can't die here. You don't have a

219

decent thing to be buried in."

Meanwhile, her radio show was due to be broadcast within days, and in her dazed mind, her worries got mixed with lines she was to say in the play. Telling her that Joyce was going to take her part didn't help. Once she was on the road to recovery, Dr. Jolanski had us laughing at the caricatures he'd drawn of us and the other nurses. Her spirits lifted even more when the play's enthusiastic directors came to tell her that the play had been so well received they intended to repeat it.

"I say, Elizabeth, it would have been better had you been there," the male lead said, which of course cheered her up still more.

While she was convalescing, everyone else was either on the sick list or not feeling so well, including Felicia and Miss Redecker, but I was feeling fine. "Miss Redecker, please put me back on the schedule."

"Thank you, but no. We will manage somehow." So, with nothing better to do, I worked on the promised two hundred Christmas gifts for Santo Tomas.

On his next trip, Coop reported that the *Teia Maru* had tied up to Pier 7 on 5 November, and that work parties from both Bilibid and Santo Tomas had spent several days unloading Red Cross supplies. The guards hadn't seemed to mind their communication with one another, and we heard that the military men were more concerned about the civilians' welfare than about their own, a phenomenon we nurses knew was typical of our Navy men. "Greetings from the American Red Cross" was boldly stamped on the tons of cases that came in, a large portion destined to be stored in Bilibid.

In other news, Coop said Japanese moviemakers were busy making two more propaganda films, one a repeat basketball game showing an enthusiastic audience on Corregidor. The other was filmed in Manila and showed U.S. Army tanks lumbering down the streets. Apparently the Japanese director had a fit when the Filipinos began tossing cigarettes and food to the American members of the cast.

"Man!" Coop said, "when a show like that leaves you pluggin' for the Japs and booin' the Yankees, you've got to admit it's high-class propaganda!"

November 15 brought a violent three-day typhoon that left Manila in shambles. The power supply was knocked out within hours, and rain coming through the holes in Bilibid's roof soon had wooden bakias floating away in the high water under the POWs' bunks. Many of the prisoners struggled to keep the stored Red Cross supplies from becoming a total loss.

Fierce winds drove ankle-deep rain into the first floor of the Big House, and parts of shanties floated away on waist-deep water in the low-lying areas. Parts of others were blown over the wall, and some were just flattened. None of the shanties escaped damage, and the upper hallways in both the Big House and the Educational Building had to house the hapless shanty dwellers.

It was bad in Los Baños, but not like that. As before, with their acetylene lamps, the men valiantly fought to save what they could. Part of the river's embankment behind the gymnasium washed away, but my garden was undamaged, thanks largely to the commandant's suggestions that I'd followed.

At the first opportunity after the storm, waiting husbands and grooms-to-be rushed over to Barracks 1 and 2, sighing with relief after seeing how well they had held up. But railroad tracks and highways had been washed out, which meant a further delay in transferring wives and sweethearts to Los Baños.

Thanksgiving 1943 passed with more lost bets on when the "Yanks and tanks" would show up. New bets were placed as the Republic of the Philippines celebrated the second anniversary of Japan's attack on Pearl Harbor.

The second transfer to Los Baños was scheduled for 10 December, and husbands and boyfriends considered it a sure thing when twelve boxcars of belongings came through the gate on 9 December. The next day, the sun was shining as the women were trucked out of Santo Tomas to the sounds of "Happy Days Are Here Again" and the wedding march.

"Welcome to Los Baños, Heidi," I said as I

passed her and Rick walking down Roosevelt Road.

"Oh, Dottie, I'm so glad to be here!" As I watched them lovingly head for their shanty, I thought about how she would not even have been in the Philippines had she not been a nurse. Only because she had agreed to respond to a call from the U.S. Army hospitals if needed, had she been allowed to accompany her husband. She had responded to Sternberg's urgent calls and had worked at the hospital in Santo Tomas, but by the time the twelve of us arrived, she had had enough of nursing.

The presence of these women brought symbols of civilization's thin veneer, things like a flourish of colorful scarfs, pieces of dulled sterling silverware, fancy salt and pepper shakers, tablecloths, centerpieces on tables here and there.

Mitch had developed close ties with several of the couples during those hectic first weeks of internment, when his optimism and positive attitude had provided a much-needed steadying factor. Naturally the new women became a part of our clique out on the lawn in the evenings, accompanying their husbands and fiancés; naturally they all had so much to talk about. With all these couples around, Father John's "He's married" began to ring repeatedly in my mind.

Meanwhile, Mitch was so involved with the newcomers that he didn't take much notice of me. I quietly left, and alone in my bed, I said the rosary a second time for good measure. I decided

I'd better break off my relationship with Mitch; I thought he would prefer it that way anyway.

My intention was to get this over with the next morning, as painlessly as possible. I would take my eating utensils out of the shanty and then pick up my chow-line breakfast. I would eat my meals here in the dormitory, then later talk about it if necessary.

But Heidi spotted me. "Dottie, dear! It's so good to see your smiling face!" she said in her usual vivacious manner. "Come eat your breakfast with us in our shanty!"

Oh, why not, I thought. But that was a mistake. Time zipped by much too fast, and before I knew it Mitch was heading toward the shanty.

"It's too early to pick up your lunch," he said, irritably taking my dishes out of my hands. "Where were you when that lousy lullaby was being played? I looked around and you were gone."

"Mitch, except for Heidi, I don't know these women. Besides, you were having such a good time talking with everyone."

"I didn't mean to shut you out," he said patronizingly as I followed him back to the shanty.

"For goodness' sake, you don't owe me a single thing!"

"Doll, what am I going to do with the likes of you?"

But for me, the question was, what am I going to do with the likes of you? Blessed Mary, you're letting me down!

It was ten days before Christmas 1943, and distraught Santo Tomas internees rushed out front where several Comfort Kits were being ripped open and spilled onto the ground. How awful it must have been to see the guards removing labels to show the English-speaking Japanese officers, who scrutinized them carefully. How awful to see those little cellophane-wrapped packages ripped open and thrown down on the dirt, little cans of meat opened and their contents dumped out.

They were doing this because they had found patriotic messages. Cigarettes were used as fillers in the Comfort Kit cases, and in a case opened in Bilibid, packages containing one particular brand carried the messages. The cigarettes were removed, to be distributed in bulk later. Finally, satisfied that nothing else in the kits contained hidden messages, the guards gave the joyful internees their Comfort Kit cases.

Cases of other supplies were opened and searched for Stateside newspapers, but the guards soon grew tired of this tedious task and some of them slipped by unnoticed. Disappointing as they were, classified ads gave imaginative clues about what was going on at home. A *New York Times* rotogravure passed the guards, and pictures of clothing worn by society ladies gave the Santo Tomas women an idea of what last year's fashions had been like.

In Los Baños as well, receiving the cases of

Comfort Kits was like hitting a jackpot. Looking back, I think they were more of a morale booster than anything else, with their small cans of Spam and Party Loaf, their packages of dried fruit, powdered milk, a fairly large chocolate candy bar, and a small container of instant coffee. Like practically everyone else, Mitch and I decided to hold on to our treasures for possible rougher times ahead.

Allen, Hank, and Dr. Foster laughed when they looked over the medical supplies. There were enough quarter-grain morphine tablets to supply all of Luzon's hospitals for the next five years! Brochures on some of the new kinds of drugs were missing, but Hank had a good idea what those manufactured by Merck and Company were and their intended use.

This year's Christmas season brought Santo Tomas internees as many emotional lows as highs. Like his predecessors on past Christmas holidays, Mr. Kato was amazed, we heard, by the large number of Filipino relatives, loyal servants, and friends who gathered at the front gate bringing even more gaily colored gifts than the year before. Considering their meager contents, recipients must have wept inwardly, knowing how much of a sacrifice it had meant to their generous people. Kato had not planned to do so, but he finally allowed short visits.

Aside from the visits, though, we heard that the celebration of Jesus' birth fell short of the joyous 1942 event with its high hopes. Our handmade gifts for the youngsters were ignored in favor of the chocolate bars in the Comfort Kits; a newly formed committee that was to make bartering and swapping items more businesslike was bypassed; the pageant staged by over a hundred students lacked enthusiasm.

Christmas in Los Baños must have been better than in any of the camps throughout the Far East. Mother Nature provided a beautiful day, and the happiness of the new arrivals was contagious. Christmas carols and church services were inspirational, and *The Philadelphia Story*, presented with self-confidence, poise, and assurance, couldn't have been better.

18

CROWDING AND CRIME

Piecemeal news about Santo Tomas and its troubles arrived with Coop, and now that Heidi was the administration committee's secretary, she was able to stay in touch with what was going on up there. Reports were that two hundred volunteers couldn't wait to be transferred to Los Baños. Our mud and rain had been a deterrent until recently, but conditions at Santo Tomas had deteriorated so badly that inclement weather was no longer an issue.

Among the new arrivals was a salty old Englishman, a former captain of a merchant ship. "Skipper Sam" fascinated listeners with his yarns about adventurous years behind the helm, before fate had dumped him and his heroic crew into the hands of the enemy.

Also among the newcomers were the two Chapman brothers. Their father had been the dean of the Agricultural College for nearly two decades, and the professor and Mrs. Chapman had remained in their on-campus residence. Now that their sons were here, they were granted permission to move into the camp. With them came their dog, the elderly Mitzi, which made Soochow no longer the only unofficial four-legged prisoner.

To the new arrivals, Los Baños was a land of milk and honey. In Santo Tomas people could no longer afford to entertain friends in their shanties, and the spirit of helping one another was all but gone. It was depressing to see so many glum people who lived in a dull world of their own making, their lifeless eyes seldom meeting those around them. Nor did they acknowledge the presence of anyone, even when bumping into a person in the crowded buildings and dining shed. But they would soon think of Los Baños as country-club living, a vibrant society filled with friendliness, fun, and laughter.

And indeed, if one had to sit out a war, this wasn't the worst way to do it. We nurses became card-carrying members of the select Gecko Chapter of the Short Snorter's Club, an idea that had originated among the last world war's servicemen. A membership card was a low denomination of money — here, a Mickey Mouse peso — on which friends and buddies signed their names.

Hospital work was as satisfying as our social life, but, with the influx of people, an extension for the hospital became necessary. What better place than our dormitory?

Dr. Foster moved from the apartment to his office, Julius back into the gymnasium, and we moved our twelve beds into the apartment, which was a masterful feat. The bedroom was a tight squeeze for the Big Three, and Lizzy, Ellen, and Bobbie had cramped spaces in the dining area. My bed was in the living room next to the front door, Amy's inches away, Velda's across the foot of ours, and Olga, Joyce, and Felicia were packed in there too.

Moving wasn't too bad with so many willing hands. Austin and his shadow dismantled Lizzy's "baha," and before long an architectural masterpiece stood next to the apartment. This one had a thatch roof that covered a much larger floor, plus additional cupboards and other amenities. It was very nice, a convenience the nurses used more frequently than her baha on the hill.

"When we get home," Ellen said, running her hand over the table's smooth surface, "we'll have to get together and go on a picnic."

"A picnic!" Liz exclaimed. "Are you out of your mind? I'm never going on another picnic as long as I live! What's more, when I get home, I never want to see the likes of any of you again!"

"Ignore her," Bobbie said. "She doesn't mean that."

"Oh, yes I do!"

Los Baños was no picnic at best, but compared with the POW camps or Santo Tomas, it was indeed country-club living here. Coop told us that Major General Morimoto, head of War Prisoners Financial Division, had started issuing orders at Santo Tomas, and that Mr. Kato was the most rattle-brained commandant yet. Lieutenant Sadaaki Konishi, the supply officer, was absolutely the most despicable man Coop had ever run across, a sloppy individual who sat around in his dirty underwear guzzling sake, picking his nose and toes, and giving orders to Mr. Kato. Rather than allow pony-drawn carretillas to take the supplies to the bodega behind the Big House, he had it dumped at the gate, which meant many trips with man-powered push carts.

It certainly was no picnic in Bilibid either, where General Morimoto had asked for a monthly analysis of the food supply. Records of what was received looked good on paper, but the hundred-pound sacks of rice were short of that weight to begin with, and closer to a third when the rocks and debris had been sorted out. Records showed that truckloads of fresh fish were brought in, but, as Bornowski entered in his log, most of it was too spoiled even for the skinny pigs. When a pig died from malnutrition at Bilibid it was slaughtered, and the meat went to the garrison's galley. The prisoners got what was left on the bones to flavor their watery rice.

We also learned that sympathizers in Manila had sent the POWs large quantities of food. They sent a thank-you note in appreciation, but it was too little too late for those who were going blind. Too late especially for those who wore, or would soon wear, a "blind man" sign written in Japanese characters. This was to protect them from being slapped for not saluting the guards.

What a pathetic sight it must have been to see these proud men in their ragged loincloths and bare feet, prisoners who saved their tattered pants, shirts, and shoes as long as possible. As hard as it was to put up with camp conditions, it must have been harder still for them to see the tear-stained faces of Filipinos watching work parties march down the streets. We were told the POWs winked at them and tried to stand tall and look as presentable as possible.

In the middle of February 1944, mail and personal packages lifted spirits. Standard-size Red Cross packages were unloaded onto the bandstand while year-old letters were being distributed. Some people got several, others got none. I got one from my mother. Following Red Cross instructions, she had written as blandly as she could. Dad was fine and hoping to paint the house soon; Paula's four-year-old son was growing so fast. But why did Mom say that Paula didn't see much of Dave anymore? He was a crazy sort of guy with his ham radio station and his love for gliders, but abandon his family? That didn't sound like him.

Then came the package. My mother sent white cotton pajamas, toothpaste, two toothbrushes, a printed blouse, underwear, and socks — all practical and appreciated.

I watched Mitch's delight as he opened his package, and the fact that he was married hit me with a bang as he said, "Well, I'll be dogged!" It was obviously a treasured pipe that he took out of his box, and with his pocketknife he began to scrape the bowl, a ritual he undoubtedly had performed so many times before.

"That should be ripe by now," Charlie chortled.

"Smells just about right," Mitch said, ceremoniously filling the pipe with aromatic tobacco. Lighting it, he looked as satisfied as if he'd been enjoying California's sunshine with his family.

Father John's "I wouldn't like to see you get hurt" screamed inside my head, and for the next few days, thinking that God had turned His back on me, I worked in the garden when Mitch wasn't around. The Blessed Mother Mary was ignoring me too, I thought, as I busied myself mending clothes, washing, ironing, doing other make-work projects, and being thoroughly miserable.

Finally he came looking for me. "Doll, you are avoiding me again. What's going on in that imaginative mind of yours?"

"I've just had so many things to do."

"Yeah, yeah, I know. Let's take a walk down Roosevelt Road and get this straightened out."

Might as well, I thought. I can't go on like this. After a few mundane comments about this and that, he wanted to know what had been bothering me. "I've been . . . well, it's something Father John said."

"Which has something to do with me?"

"I would say so."

"Does he object to married men having women friends? You have men friends who are married, and many of my friends are married women. Is

233

there anything wrong with that?"

"You're missing the point. It's just that . . . that . . ."

"That what?"

"Mitch, you are a good friend. I like you very much. You know that, but . . ."

"Are you trying to tell me you want to break up our friendship?"

"It's . . . it's just that . . . that . . ."

Mitch said nothing, but waited patiently as we walked on.

Finally I said, "Father John warned me about letting myself get hurt. Do you understand what I'm saying?"

"Dottie, doll," he said and, pulling my arm under his, he held my hand in both of his while he thought this out. "By chance, you and I have been thrown together in this miserable internment camp. You could say it's an interlude in our lives, an enforced pause in time until we can put our lives back together." He looked at my hand as though it were a treasured item. "Making your life a little happier gives me a sense of purpose. Can you understand that?" I didn't answer.

"You are a restful person to be around," he went on. "I like to be with you, to orbit around you, to . . . one of these days our armed forces will be coming back. It's going to be a helluva fight."

As he held my hand, I felt his warmth. Several moments passed before he added, "Doll, has it ever occurred to you that we may not come out of this alive?"

That possibility had been in the back of my mind right from the beginning of the war, but it wasn't dying that troubled me right now. It was the idea of cutting off the strong affinity that had developed between Mitch and me, and I began to cry.

"I'm sorry," he said, "I didn't mean to upset you." In his arms, I could hear his comforting heartbeat, and eventually it calmed me.

When I stopped blubbering, he wiped away the tears and said, "Here, let me look at you. You are such a pretty thing."

"Oh, I can imagine that!" I couldn't help but laugh.

Oh, dear Jesus, Mary, and Joseph, I thought. Oh, merciful God in Heaven! It would be easier to chop off my right arm than to give up my relationship with Mitch. You *do* understand, don't you?

Even our meticulous chief nurse had a beau; Skipper Sam made her smile and laugh because she really felt like it. She did have emotional problems, though. She had been able to tolerate Room 30A fairly well, but here, the apartment's tight quarters nearly drove her over the edge. All the more so because except for Liz, Olga, and Felicia, the word *meticulous* to the rest of us meant neatly disorganized to sloppy.

Amy and I were glad our beds were next to the

front door; through the window we could enjoy the peaceful outside scene. But we couldn't block out the biting and nasty comments that came up from time to time.

"Amy, I'd sure like to move into one of the barracks."

"I'll go with you."

"Do you mean that? Really?"

She did, and I rushed over to see if Heidi could pull a few strings.

"Oh, Dottie, dear! Before any of these apartment-hunting newlyweds take it, I'll put your names on just the right one!"

It was in Barracks 2, the cubicle in the southwest corner, almost directly across the road from the hospital. Charlie's noisy flushing invention was far enough away so that it wouldn't bother us and, most important, our beds and belongings left plenty of heavenly space.

Cubicles in Barracks 1 and 2 were separated by wood paneling, not sawali, like most of the others. Each had a door from the building's long center hallway and an outside door, where we could set up a little patio.

The siding, same as the nipa-covered roof, kept the barracks cool in the summer and warm in the winter. With no attics, it had no bats as did the dormitory. We decided that if we didn't bother the beady-eyed lizards running back and forth under the roof, they wouldn't bother us.

The main kitchen and its bodega were in the next building, but it was easier for us to adjust to the sound of banging utensils and the noisy kitchen crew than to that bickering in the apartment.

The Japanese barracks were hidden behind a sawali fence, thank heavens. But at precisely seven o'clock in the morning, the guards would be out on Roosevelt Road, growling and grunting unintelligibly, their hands clapping over their heads then hitting their thighs as two hundred pairs of heavy boots landed on the macadamized road in unison.

Happily for the hospital's apartment dwellers, Felicia moved into another cubicle with Helena, and Velda into one with a civilian woman she had befriended.

From what we heard, now that General Morimoto had taken over supplying Santo Tomas, the number of guards carrying bayoneted rifles had doubled at the camp's gates. Blackout regulations and air-raid drills had been put into effect both there and at Bilibid where, so it seemed, the victorious Japanese army could no longer afford to be anything approaching magnanimous.

On 7 April, five hundred and thirty internees arrived from Santo Tomas.

"Holy Toledo, they've sent us all of their criminals, whores, thugs and thieves, not to mention the near-sick, the mentally sick, and the socially unwanted!"

"Can you believe it? There's that crummy Cheiver, still looking like a woman with his long hair, still in the same dirty white pajamas and slippers."

Rowdy kids meant no more peace and quiet at Los Baños, and with them came Gerty, Mario, Maxie the no-good beachcomber, and other misfits. All of it spelled trouble ahead.

These bums stampeded the canteen on Tuesday when it opened. Mario immediately bought tobacco at twenty pesos a kilo, and quadrupled its cost to buyers in Santo Tomas.

"They told us we wouldn't have to work down here," some claimed, and of course, the hospital clinic had a steady flow of hypochondriacs, including the beachcomber. Dr. Foster's patience was sorely tried with so many goldbrickers. And then there were those who were more dead than alive, and the hospital's extension had to be extended.

The pump couldn't fill the reservoir fast enough, and the water had to be shut off to most areas except for two hours a day, not because the camp was being wasteful.

Meanwhile, in the midst of all this, there was still Mitch and me. Just to look at one another was comforting, something that didn't go unnoticed. "You two make such a darling couple," romantic Heidi said, and whispered, "I think he loves you."

"As though I were his sister," I whispered back.

But let tomorrow take care of itself, I thought. For today, Mitch and I each knew we were important to someone special, something that made the days easier to bear.

This group of internees had more than its share of lawbreakers, and Gerrad's discipline committee was rightfully upset, as was Mr. Caldwell.

"Take it easy Gerrad, we can't stand around with a club in our hands."

"Hell, they're stealing everything they can get their hands on. Not only are they cutting windows in the barracks, they're helping themselves to the camp's garden, pulling eggplants and everything else right out of the ground!"

Mario offered a Japanese officer a commission for selling jewelry, and the commandant demanded that he be *justly* punished. Mario laughed at the sixty-day jail sentence, but he became thoroughly enraged when Caldwell told him a detailed record of his conduct would be turned over to an American military court as soon as possible.

Gerrad's committee then started an all-out crackdown, and light-weight offenders had to be jailed like anyone else. Andrew, of Harvard extract, thought the whole affair was an exciting drama. "Hey, Mitch, don't you think Gerrad's men are going overboard?"

"Where should he draw the line, Andy? How can he be lenient with some and not with the others?"

It was soon mayhem. They were stealing from the Japanese contractor in broad daylight, and Gerrad's men hid behind bushes waiting to catch someone taking a drink of liquor.

Mitch agreed that Gerrad was going too far.

"But doggone it, without respect for laws, we would rightly deserve the jungle life we could be living. What would you have Gerrad do? What would you have me do? Turn the whole bunch loose? If we do it for one, we will have to do it for the others."

Weeks turned into months. Mitch remained chairman of the board of judges, whose membership grew to include another three men and one woman. The camp was getting fairly well organized. But then one day, Charlie showed up with news.

"Are you ready for this? It'll jar your teeth loose," he said. "You ready?"

"Not if it's another one of those lousy rumors you make up."

"Ah, to hell with you, Mitch," said Charlie, turning to leave.

"Tell us," Mitch said tolerantly. "What's going to jar our teeth loose?"

"Lieutenant Sadaaki Konishi moved into Barracks 4."

19

DEPRIVATIONS

Our hospital and its extensions were nearly full, and I regularly sought refuge behind the shanty — mentally tired and physically exhausted. So sick of so much to do and so little to do it with. Sick of unappreciative civilians who seemed to think the world owed them a living. Sick of so much bitching and gossiping in Barracks 2.

Break loose, you silly old bridge, so I can see you fall into the roaring river. It didn't, of course.

The garden was no longer just a hobby or a pleasant retreat; it was getting to be a necessity, now that Konishi was here. It was doing well enough that Mitch and I could still share its yield, but if only the corn would grow as fast as the greens, I thought. Heaven knows we all have lost too much weight already. Olga had pinned up the seams in both of my uniforms and Julia had sewn them, bless them both.

The scarcity of food had become such a problem that individual gardens were in demand. Available land was surveyed and a drawing was held for the remaining little plots.

Thankfully, there was no shortage of morphine,

241

which came with the Red Cross supplies. Without it, general anesthesia would have been more than we could have handled.

But it wasn't only pain we had to contend with; as time went by, death was no longer a stranger in Los Baños. More and more of our old-timers began to die. They were buried respectfully in an alloted cemetery plot around the chapel.

Then two young people died. At age eighteen, Angela shouldn't have died. It was as though some demonic force had created a hormonal, metabolic, or endocrine imbalance that changed her too-thin body into obesity. With acute appendicitis, a postoperative infection was ninety-nine percent guaranteed. Dr. Foster had no choice but to remove the appendix nevertheless, and hope for the best. We all worked around the clock, but to no avail. Angela died, and the camp wept.

Next came Oliver, seventeen. Although Los Baños was in a malaria belt, surprisingly few internees picked it up here. Why should this befall Oliver? It did, and it was his undoing as the protozoan parasites in his blood invaded the meningeal membranes of his brain. We all worked desperately to keep him alive. Dr. Foster spent sleepless nights at his bedside, but it was not enough, and again the camp wept.

"Geez, these things come in threes. Someone else is going to die."

"Joyce, don't say that!" But someone else did die.

Maxie the beachcomber had been a plague to the clinic from the minute he'd arrived. No one knew much about him, only that he was obnoxious, but where he was from and how he happened to be in the Philippines in the first place was hard to say, since no one had bothered to ask.

Dr. Foster had impatiently seen him for his stomach ache, headache, backache, indigestion, joint aches, and on down the list of complaints, but having no apparent reason for a Wasserman lab test, he had missed the hidden syphilitic symptoms between the secondary and tertiary stages.

Maxie shouldn't have died, but he did. No tears were shed, but oppressive feelings of guilt hung over the heartless and unfeeling camp for days.

The dead had to be buried right away, but Maxie died on a Saturday, and the Jewish internees refused to compromise. As a result, his coffin was not carried respectfully to the cemetery; it was taken there on the kitchen cart. No one attended his funeral because there was none. Father John was there to help dig and then shovel the dirt back into the grave, and undoubtedly the only prayers said on Maxie's behalf were Catholic.

In a dry spell, sitting out on the lawn with our little group, listening to the PA recordings and visiting, Heidi and I lost interest in what the men were talking about, and complimented Diane on the beautiful concert she and her violinist friend Alice had given.

"You two were so pretty in your evening gowns. You played so well," Heidi said.

"Oh, yes," I added. "The bandstand was beautifully decorated. The lighting was just right, and I must say, it took me thousands of miles out of here."

The piano was stored in the end of the barracks where Protestant services were held, and that was where the two musicians practiced. Sometimes Diane would lose herself from camp life as her fingers ran over the keyboard, softly or vigorously, as suited her mood. When Alice was freed from her motherly duties, the two of them spent many hours there, if only for mental relaxation.

One day they were playing a rather intricate piece when a surly faced guard came in and scared the wits out of them. They continued nervously to play until they were stopped. "You play Johann Strauss 'Blue Danube'," he ordered.

This they did, relaxing somewhat with its waltz rhythm. In future visits, they became less anxious about his presence, knowing that he was an accomplished cellist in one of Japan's favored orchestras. They were reluctant to accept his food gifts of appreciation, but with Konishi chipping away at the food supply, it was too hard to resist.

Other well-educated Japanese guards also enjoyed the finer things in life and liked to visit with the Americans. But, as friendly as most were, they wouldn't have hesitated to shoot an internee or a prisoner if their emperor had expected that of them.

As a prelude to Brahms' "Lullaby" one night, an announcement on the PA system was made: "One hundred volunteers will be needed to help bring in four hundred civilians from the train station tomorrow morning. Be ready to leave at 10:30 after an early lunch."

This was a tedious task on this hot, humid, and muggy day, and it was nearly three o'clock before the wretched people began coming through the gate. It turned out to be several Catholic groups, and they got a frosty reception from the internees, who knew they had signed an agreement with the Japanese Army of Occupation in order to remain free. The agreement was that they would neither interfere with the Japanese military nor give aid to the Allies.

The Japanese had taken them quite by surprise; some had less than three hours' notice, none more than twenty-four hours. Other than beds and bedding, their personal effects were limited, and they stood confused and helpless until they were led to "Vatican City," in the upper level of the camp. The lower level, where the rest of us were, would now be called "Hell's Half Acre."

20

U.S. PLANES SPOTTED

In August 1944, two things happened to brighten my month. Clara returned the yarn I gave her in the form of a beautiful sweater. It was only waist length and the sleeves hardly covered my elbows, but it was the most useful sweater I ever had.

A second event started out as a worrisome one. My period was three weeks overdue, and since Bobbie had had a hysterectomy, I wondered if I, too, could be developing tumors.

"Do you have a reason to be worried?" she asked when I told her.

"Oh, come on!"

As we talked, I was amazed to learn that I had continued to menstruate longer than the other nurses. In fact, nearly all the women in camp had stopped this troublesome problem, a blessing in disguise, we decided.

On the gloomy side, Konishi made this muddy month worse as he continued to hack away at the food issued to the camp. What had been six caldrons of cornmeal mush for breakfast was reduced to four, and to make enough to go around, ground rice was added. Currently, the daily menu

246

consisted of ersatz coffee at 7:30, cornmeal mush with coconut milk at 10:30, and a questionable supper at 4:00.

The canteen ran out of everything in short order when the camp was told that everyone's money was to be turned in to the commandant. Unlike in military camps, adults were to be paid 50 pesos a month, children 25 pesos, and the rest of the funds were to be set aside for heaven only knew what.

For our Los Baños haves, losing the power of money was painful. As for the have-nots, you would have thought they were the only ones suffering. For us, it was money we wouldn't otherwise have had, and we hoped the canteen would continue to have something to spend it on.

August gave way to September, but the passage of time had no healing effect on Mitch. He couldn't conceal his disillusionment in the self-centered attitude of some of the camp's most needed citizens, not that he was about to voluntarily give up his chairmanship on the board of judges, nor did anyone ask him to do so. Instead, he focused his anger on Konishi by putting in more time at his job than it warranted. He checked and signed for food received from the Filipinos at the gate, signed for the sacks of rice, cornmeal, salt, and like items issued from the Japanese bodega, rationed the food out to the hospital and main kitchens, and helped the head cook plan the menu.

As for Konishi, the physical setup here did not lend itself to the numerous petty harassments he had inflicted on the internees in Santo Tomas, but he still managed to get his pittance of humility. He would order five or six hundred sacks of supplies moved from the Japanese bodega into the camp's bodega, then order it moved back again. The second time he did this the internees went on strike, and the guards moved the supplies back.

Sometimes Konishi would say four or five hundred kilos of camotes, mongo beans, or other supplies were to be delivered. The kitchen crew would prepare to handle that amount, and only a hundred kilos would come in, usually with part of it unsalvageable. Sad Sadaaki's sake-saturated mind may have found all this amusing.

Previously, men worked in the gardens because they enjoyed it, and if they took a few green vegetables to bolster their own menu, no one objected. Now that the two gardens couldn't produce enough to fill the camp's needs, they were criticized. So too were the cooks, who made sure their own liberal helpings were set aside before the camp was served.

Rick was on the coconut-milk detail, but he quit because he didn't want his name associated with those who weren't taking just a little extra. They not only took a little for themselves, they were trading it for canned goods.

Complaints were many, but mild compared to those in Manila. Coop seldom made shuttle-bus trips these days, and we had to depend on getting news from Santo Tomas through the grapevine or the bamboo telegraph. Supposedly blackout regulations had been issued in Manila and air-raid practices continued in both Bilibid and Santo Tomas, and the guards in both places had dug foxholes for themselves.

Internees at Santo Tomas and POWs in Bilibid were accustomed to seeing the Japanese pilots shoot at a tow-plane's target, but on 21 September they were startled when one of the practicing planes exploded in midair. After that came waves of American planes that finished off the rest of the exercising Japanese planes. The Americans dropped bombs on the nearby airfields and, with machine guns roaring, they dove down and out of sight along the waterfront. Zooming skyward again, they left their targets in flames. This spectacular two-hour show was repeated again in the afternoon, and twice again on the next day.

At the same time, we in Los Baños wondered what the guards were looking at in the distance. The orderlies and I went up to the hospital balcony, from where we too could watch this unusual air show. Soon the entire on-duty staff had joined us.

A battling U.S. Hellcat and a Japanese Zero were far enough away so that their dogfight maneuvering seemed no more than practicing. But then antiaircraft puffs of smoke began peppering the sky, and the Zero exploded! The commandant frantically peddled his bicycle up Roosevelt

Road, and when the confused guards donned their helmets and jumped around with fixed bayonets, we knew those flights off in the distance *had* to be American planes!

Bong! Bong! Bong! went Charlie's cowboy-style triangle, which he'd made out of old pipe. The garden detail was chased back to their barracks, and monitors yelled for their wards to go into their cubicles.

"They're back! They're back!"

"Hundreds and hundreds of them!"

"It's about time they came to get us out of here!"

All of us were laughing, crying, and dancing around in juvenile giddiness.

Most of the repeat performances were too far north for our Los Baños observers to see, but suddenly a low-flying Hellcat in distress zoomed across the sky, not that we could tell whose plane it was. Before it disappeared over the mountain, its pilot could be seen coming down in a parachute.

Off in the distance the evening sky glowed in delicate yellow and orange colors. Suddenly it brightened and vibrations from a blast could be felt. What was that? A fuel-storage tank? An ammunition dump?

"It won't be long now!" someone shouted gleefully.

But on the following evening, although the night sky glowed the show was over, and wagers had to be settled.

Our garden workers had been betting on when the Americans would bomb Luzon. One of the two Dutch priests working with them had bet on 21 September, and the two priests walked away with twenty cans of corned beef.

"He must be an oracle of some kind," the internees said reverently. "He's getting help from upstairs."

But there was no help from upstairs when an official Japanese party spent a week at the camp. Those who optimistically thought this was for the camp's benefit soon found out how wrong they were. The YMCA building was to be made into a Japanese field hospital, and, except for our hospital, all the other original camp's buildings were to be temporary quarters for transient Japanese troops.

October 9, 1944
By order of the Commandant, including the YMCA, all buildings north of Mac- Arthur Boulevard are to be vacated by Saturday, October 14th.
Further details will be posted soon.
J. M. Caldwell, Chairman
Administration Committee

They were cutting our fifty-five acres in half in five days' time, and the enormous task ahead was bewildering. A year ago such a move would have been loudly protested, but gone were the days of country club living, when it had been a pleasure for the men to work up a sweat. Hunger had become as chronic here as it had long been for the military prisoners, and the internees found it didn't take much exercise to leave one breathless.

A new order read, "All shelves, cupboards and anything attached to the buildings are to remain."

"Poetic justice, wouldn't you say? Those were made from the Jap contractor's lumber."

No matter, the devil himself must have been laughing at us as a steady drizzle turned the grounds into a quagmire. It was hard enough for the aged to stand in line for their supper, much less walk across the street, but they had no choice. With their possessions, they trudged up Roosevelt Road along with the others, slipping and falling in the mud, until they finally found their way to their new home.

"Look at those damned missionaries," some grumbled, "standing there with their arms folded. Can't they see these old codgers are in trouble?"

Patients and equipment in the hospital's dormitory extension had to be carried to a new location, and what would we ever have done without the additional orderlies and nurses' aides?

Camp-bought food supplies, a precious but dwindling hedge against a shaky future, were moved from the YMCA to the camp's bodega. Shanties had to be dismantled. It took several men to move the nipa roofs up the road, and soon Vatican City was cluttered beyond belief.

"You are welcome to anything in my garden," I told the nurses. Amy and I replanted as much as we could outside our cubicle, but the roots hardly had a chance to take hold before someone had spirited them away.

According to Bornowski's daily log, on 10 October 1944 he was ordered to compile a list of able-bodied prisoners, "able-bodied" meaning anyone who could walk. The 1,685 names on this list included Commander Walters, the Navy's entire medical staff, eligible POWs in Bilibid, and those to be brought in from Cabanatuan and other outlying areas. These men were to be shipped to Japan, and they knew it.

Starting on 15 October, air raids over the Manila Bay area went on almost daily, too far away from Los Baños for us to see anything more than the comforting flights off in the distance.

On 20 October the grapevine told us that General MacArthur had made a radio broadcast from Tacloban: "I have returned." As much as I wanted to believe it, I would have to put that on a back burner, I decided. Still, we couldn't help but know that something big was going on down south.

Perhaps other Navy prisoners had forgotten that 27 October was Navy Day, but we nurses felt certain that something exciting would happen on that day. The only noteworthy event turned out to be the birth of a scrawny baby, a cute little doll who cried in protest as she entered this miserable barbed-wire world.

On 30 October Army doctors and corpsmen took over Bilibid's hospital, but Bornowski and five other Navy technicians were to remain. The new senior medical officer instructed Bornowski to turn all Navy records over to him, but as far as Bornowski was concerned, with his own copy safely hidden, the records had been ordered by the Japanese and would be turned over only to them.

In November some Bilibid prisoners were shuffled off to Nielson airfield, and those whose names were on the list dreaded what was to come.

In Los Baños, one of the nuns was caught gathering a few green onions from the garden next to the piggery. "This is Dr. Foster's garden," Julius said coldly.

"Oh, I didn't know that," she said nervously, and making the sign of the cross, she gave him the onions and hurried off to her quarters.

Dr. Foster was fit to be tied. Others who said they had seen the sisters in his garden before merely added fuel to his indignation, and he was steaming mad.

The offending sister's Mother Superior asked that the guilty culprit identify herself, which she did, and the entire group of sisters went to the doctor to apologize. "Your conduct is inexcusable!" Dr. Foster shouted at them. "You women are a disgrace to your order and to the Catholic Church, and by God, I'll see you in court!"

In the hospital, he made loud comments to the Catholic nurses, including me.

"I feel so bad about the sisters," Lizzy nervously told me. "They thought I needed fresh green vegetables, bless them, and they only brought a few at a time. I certainly didn't ask them to do this. I don't know where they got them. Oh, they said something about working in the gardens, but —"

"For heaven's sake, Liz, you don't need to defend them or yourself to me. Honestly, the way the doctor is acting, you'd think a murder had been committed."

The upcoming trial was the talk of the camp. As far as most of the internees were concerned, it was the doctor's garden and those parasitic sisters had no business being there. The doctor's worth was recognized by all. During all his time in Los Baños, he had been the only medical-surgical doctor. He had been on call day and night, not that he had generally been overworked. He had professionally and gratuitously seen most of the internees at one time or another, and they probably felt as indebted to him as I did.

"You're not going to the trial?" Lizzy asked me anxiously.

"Not me. I'll get all the sordid details soon enough."

"Will you keep an eye on the clinic? I'm a material witness."

"Are you really?" I couldn't help but laugh, but it wasn't funny to her as she rushed to join the big turnout, come to see that justice was done.

"I, Father Markham, am representing the sisters."

"Very well," Mitch said, and the court clerk made a note of that.

"Dr. Foster, is someone representing you?"

"Hell, no!" he yelled. "I'll represent myself!"

"Very well, would you like to state your case?"

The doctor glared at the bevy of sisters clustered around their Mother Superior. He scathingly denounced them all for the dastardly deed of stealing his onions, claiming that such behavior on their part was inexcusable, and, by God, it had to be stopped.

Father Markham stated that the defendant thought that section was a part of the camp's garden, and that she did not know it belonged to Dr. Foster. Witnesses were called to the stand. Legalese dialogue went on until all points were covered, all except one. The defense again called Julius to the stand.

"Mr. Cohen," Father Markham said, "please identify the sister in question."

He looked at each sister carefully. "They all look alike to me," he said. "I can't tell one from the other."

"Case dismissed," Mitch yelled immediately, and gaveled the table with a resounding bang.

The doctor was furious. He yelled at Julius, at Mitch, at Father Markham. The sisters trembled as he angrily accused them of being anything but Christian . . . at least that's the way I heard it.

21

WAITING

As the days of November slipped by, we couldn't help realizing that something important was happening beyond the now-double rows of barbed wire. Where and what exactly it was we didn't know, but MacArthur's "I have returned" message stayed in our minds, loud and clear. Most encouraging were sights and sounds of aircraft off in the distance, and detonations that made the ground tremble.

"They're probably shelling the Batangas coast," Charlie said.

"Must be," Mitch said. "Filipinos at the gate say regiments of Jap troops have been heading north."

"All we need now is a survival kit."

"Okay, what's a survival kit?"

"It has gin, vermouth, and green olives, and as soon as you put them all together, some Yankee jackass out there's gonna show up to tell you that's not the way to mix a martini."

The Japanese were making an ammunition dump in Santo Tomas, bringing in crates of submachine guns and ammunition and stacking them in front of the Educational Building. With tents set up, the out-of-bounds area looked like a military fort. Japanese guards took over the entire first floor and part of the second floor of the Educational Building, and we heard that Mr. Kato began to drive everyone crazy with his snooping around, giving orders and then counterorders that made no sense.

We also heard that a secreted copy of the no-longer-issued *Manila Tribune* had made its way into Santo Tomas. Supposedly, a notice on the last page gave the departure date for the Red Cross ship in Vladivostok and its arrival date in Manila. By the time this choice bit of news reached Los Baños, descriptions of the "72-pound" Comfort Kits were phenomenal.

At least the prospect of another Red Cross supply ship coming in was nice to think about. So was the hope that Major Iwanata, our new senior officer, would improve matters concerning supply officer Sadaaki Konishi.

This time, the hateful creature had our sacks of salt moved from the camp's bodega to the garrison's, and he issued a daily ration of only six grams for the entire camp. This was to be the rate of issue for the duration.

All foods have some degree of salt, so generally speaking, this wasn't life-threatening in itself. But salt helps to retain body fluid, so the lack of it resulted in long lines for the toilet facilities. Other than tasteless food and temporary irritability, it probably did little physical damage. For those with chronic diarrhea and dysentery, it could possibly have created a metabolic alkalosis, and for those already close to dying, the lack of salt could have been a final push.

But we were becoming more and more aware of what real hunger was all about. As the spokeswoman for a group of protesting women, Gerty was the only one Konishi would listen to as, perched on his desk and filing her fingernails, she stated her mission. For that night's meal, and that one only, the ration was increased. Not by much.

A delegation from Vatican City went to the commandant, Mr. Ito, with a plea for more food, but this was in the hands of the supply officer, they were told. Meanwhile there was less than ever, and no more coconuts.

We nurses were glad we had something meaningful to do. Without a worthwhile incentive, many lethargic people were too sick to do anything for themselves, and the Comfort Kits couldn't get here any too soon.

After Thanksgiving, around two hundred internees were sent from Santo Tomas to Los Baños — the nonproductive who were over fifty years of age. About two-thirds volunteered, thinking the food situation would be better here.

Being cheerful wasn't easy, but I made it a point to put on an optimistic front, especially for our patients. Along with the other nurses, I cared, and they knew it.

Mitch made it easier, too. His angry feelings toward Konishi helped him keep his blood pressure up, as did his efforts to maintain some kind of law and order. But, I had to ask myself, who in the outside world could possibly give a hoot in hell about what went on in this godforsaken internment camp?

On 13 December prisoners were stuffed into the holds of the *Oryoko Maru*, according to Bornowski's private journal. Through sub-rosa information from one of the sentries, he learned that the ship that departed on 14 December was bombed and strafed, and survivors were taken to the Bataan coast. The Japanese took a large amount of clothing, food, and medicines, presumably for these men. On 21 December, according to unofficial information, these prisoners of war again departed for Japan.

Internees in Los Baños began to talk about food incessantly. Exchanging recipes became a social event of sorts, where likes and dislikes of different kinds of foods were discussed. Simple and exotic dishes were covered casually, and hours were spent looking at scrapbooks of pictures of food and recipes cut out of prewar magazines. The guards encouraged us to believe that Comfort Kits would show up any time now.

Young children drew pictures of foods they had heard of but had never seen or tasted. Thoughts of chocolate bars sent them into fantasyland. Comfort Kits had them, and Comfort Kits would be here any day now. Of this, believers were sure.

But for Mitch, wishing wouldn't bring back the

cigarettes that were gone, or the coffee and almost everything else he and I had tried to save. "Doll, do you know that some of these lunatics are hoping the Americans don't take over until after the Comfort Kits are here?"

As each day passed, visions of Comfort Kits loomed astronomically. The believers had never wanted anything so badly. They knew the kits were right here in Los Baños, and why weren't they being released? Mr. Caldwell tried to discourage this thinking, but to satisfy them he made an inquiry.

"Comfort Kits?" Mr. Ito asked, surprised that the ruse had lasted so long. "I assure you, there have been no Red Cross supplies brought into the Far East since last year."

On 22 and 23 December, it was easy to find volunteers to bring five hundred sacks of rice into the camp. Konishi let it be known that at the rate it was now being consumed, this would last about three months. But he didn't mention that the largest share would be used by the garrison.

Another camp garden was finally granted, in a rock-filled area. Without fertilizer and insecticides, the weak little plants that popped out didn't have a chance. Konishi asked the gardeners to work five-hour shifts and, as an incentive, he offered them an extra two hundred grams of uncooked rice to do so. This came from the camp's supply, and sake-fortified Konishi again got his daily pittance of humility.

Soon it would be my third internment Christmas, and it promised to be the most dismal day yet. But then, on the afternoon before Christmas, Vatican City put on a songfest. Before long almost everyone showed up, and for well over an hour the priests and sisters sang songs that were neither proselytizing nor mushy. They were sentimental favorites that brought visions of home and tears to our hearts if not to our eyes. Lively foot-tapping tunes induced us to join in on the singing, and best of all were the funny parodies that had us laughing and cheering.

> We'll be going to . . . Leyte,
> When the war is through . . . Leyte,
> A short ride on the train,
> Shipboard once again,
> Through the ocean lane.
> To Leyte, Leyte.
> Skies are always fair in Leyte,
> And we will all be there, in Leyte,
> Not in Mindanao,
> Not in old Davao,
> Not in Surigao,
> But Leyte!
>
> Hi diddle dee de!
> Next month we will be free!
> The day will dawn so bright and fair,
> We'll look for the guards and they won't be
>   there.
> Hi diddle dee dum!

Somebody's day is done!
We'll peek in the gym and we'll find Marines
With barrels of pork and a ton of beans
A'cooking for all the Philippines,
And then we will be free!

Everyone loved it. The dim view of the religious groups softened considerably, and at long last they were accepted by their fellow internees.

Midnight mass was conducted in the barracks chapel, and nearly as many non-Catholics as Catholics attended. In its simplicity, the altar was beautiful in the candlelight. A remarkable nativity scene featured figures that had been fashioned by a master sand sculptor, and the sisters sang carols as well as the mass. This celebration of the birth of Christ would turn out to be the most meaningful I would ever know.

"Merry Christmas," Mitch said the next morning, and apologized for not properly wrapping a Christmas present for me. What a treasure! The prized Hope diamond was worthless compared with this entire roll of toilet paper, but where had he gotten it? Mitch dickering with a Japanese guard? Not likely, but what had happened to his almost-dry fountain pen?

Christmas Day itself was like none any of us could have hoped for. Gifts came from the heart in the form of a sincere clasping of hands, a meeting of eyes, a hug, a smile that said all is well.

General George Kenney's Army Air Force presented a gift of its own: a dramatic show, as hundreds of bombers and fighters roared overhead!

With a little urging, Amy agreed to join Mitch and me for a Christmas dinner, and we laughed hilariously at our efforts to fry lugao in facial cold cream. We chopped up the upi, a strange squash-like vegetable that a Filipino at the gate had slipped to Mitch, and with much ado, out came our last can of Party Loaf.

"Merry Christmas!" Andy yelled gaily as he passed by in his bakias, shorts from made-over slacks, a tattered white shirt, and of all things, a black bow tie!

The days after Christmas were truly down, down, down. Meager servings from the main kitchen did little for empty stomachs, and as much as Mr. Ito had firmly objected, he made no further attempt to stop the trafficking that went on between the soldiers and the internees.

New Year's Eve came, and only those on the night shift bothered to exchange greetings. Drugs and medical supplies were all but gone, and our patients got little more than concerned nursing care and friendly smiles. Long gone was the crude camp-manufactured soap, impossible to make without lard or coconut oil, and the hospital was farther than ever from an aseptic haven. Gum from the one rubber tree was no longer available since it, too, had been chopped down for fire-

264

wood. Now there was nothing in the way of an adhesive to hold dressings in place.

"Do the best you can," Miss Redecker urged, brightly adding, "Those are *our* planes out there!"

But despite our efforts, the camp's death rate climbed. Charlie's crew had trouble making enough coffins to meet the needs, much less finding men strong enough to dig the holes and carry the dead to the cemetery.

Then Skipper Sam died. This was different. To everyone, he was extra special. The children loved him. They were all members of his crew, his "maties," and he had taught them to handle their own problems.

From the day he had been admitted to the hospital until the day he died, Miss Redecker was at his side. Dr. Foster operated on him hoping to stop his internal bleeding, but the Skipper's starved body was too weak to respond. He shouldn't have died with the war's end so close.

We had never before seen Miss Redecker cry. Tears welled uncontrollably in her eyes as, dazed, she wandered about his room, moving a chair a few inches, wiping imaginary dust off a shelf, reluctant to leave yet knowing there was nothing left for her to do. The sheet-covered body would be picked up. It would be put into a coffin and carried off to the cemetery to be buried by a grieving community.

22

CAMP FREEDOM
DESTROYED

"Dottie, wake up," Amy whispered. "It's almost midnight, and something strange is going on outside." Jumping out of bed, we sneaked out into the shadows in front of Barracks 2. From there we saw several trucks and the commandant's sedan in front of the Japanese barracks. It looked as though something was being loaded into them.

Seeing two of the guards heading down the road toward us, we jumped back into our cubicle. One of them went on to Barracks 1; the one who came into our barracks stopped at the monitor's door, talked to him briefly, then left.

Within the hour, forty-seven shovels were taken to Barracks 4. At 3:30 A.M., the administration committee members were called to Barracks 3, there to find the Japanese packing their belongings, sorting and burning papers, and frantically scurrying around.

"By sudden order from superiors," Mr. Ito said, "we release internees at five o'clock to administration committee. You will be in complete

266

charge of camp." He paused to speak to Major Iwanata, who then gave Mr. Caldwell the funds that had been collected from the internees months ago.

"We leave food provisions. Will last two months if used wisely. Suggest committee keep all internees inside the camp. By our orders, in one hour we leave. That is all I want to tell you."

But according to Heidi, that wasn't all he had to say. She was called out to type a list of all the internees' names, not easy on an old typewriter with a tired sheet of carbon paper. The commandant wanted the original for himself; the copy was for the administration committee. He also wanted an official statement signed by Mr. Caldwell, one stating that on this date, 9 January 1945, the camp had officially been turned over to him and his administration committee.

By now the whole camp was awake, and Caldwell couldn't broadcast his pleas for order fast enough. As soon as the last vehicle left the gate, neither he nor Gerrad's discipline committee could prevent the swarms of once lethargic internees from raiding Barracks 3 and 4. Mattresses, buckets, tools, chairs, tables, anything they could get their hands on was carted away.

At 6:30, Mr. Caldwell addressed the camp and explained what had happened. He told the internees that he had gone over to Major Iwanata's office with the shovels to see what was going on.

"Konishi had a wet towel around his head and a bottle of sake on the table." This brought gales of laughter. "He was packing his personal belongings, and believe it or not, he was having huge bales of Mickey Mouse money hauled out to be loaded on the trucks!" Caldwell went on to relate what Ito had said, word for word, and cautioned the internees about leaving the confines of the camp. "And, ladies and gentlemen, as of five o'clock this morning, your committee declared this Camp Freedom!" Applause with whoops and hollers followed.

"I must forewarn you, though. First, we do not know if landings have actually been made on Luzon. It is known, however, that our forces are on Marinduque Island, south of us. Second, we have no reason to believe that the Japanese have abandoned this area. Consequently the camp is probably still in a war zone and subject to all the dangers and risks of actual warfare.

"The administration committee will continue to be responsible until the camp is officially under control of the American Army. We ask that everyone remain calm and maintain the same camp organization as has existed. Let me remind you that this may be the most difficult period of our internment, and the fullest cooperation of every one of you is earnestly requested.

"At sunrise, there will be a simple flag-raising ceremony in front of Barracks 15. We certainly do not want enemy retaliation, and the flags will almost immediately be lowered."

He reiterated the dangers of going out of the camp, then his eyes lighted as he made his final statement. "Breakfast will be served at 8:30, lunch at 12:30, and dinner at 5:00 with full rations for all!"

At seven o'clock in the morning, the entire internee body assembled outside Barracks 15, where a makeshift bamboo flagpole had been set up. An Episcopal bishop lead the group in the Lord's Prayer, then said, "And let us say a prayer of thanksgiving, and a prayer for those who have given and are giving their lives in the struggle now going on."

We all stood at attention and watched tearfully as an American flag was raised to the top of the pole. It was an electrifying moment as we sang "The Star Spangled Banner."

The American flag was replaced by England's along with their national anthem, then it too was lowered. I never did find out who managed to hang onto the flags, but thank God somebody did!

This was a day of rejoicing, yet also one of dread and fear of what might lie ahead. Despite the warnings, daring internees lost no time in going out the gate and into the countryside. Local Filipinos came over, eager to exchange food for clothing that they needed so desperately. Other than saving something to wear home and Paul's jacket, I gladly offered all I had.

While I was fishing through my trunk, the worrisome "You and your damned *Houston*" letter fell out of the dictionary Harriet had returned to me in the Cañacao Nurses Quarters! Had I known it was there, I might not have felt so guilty these past three years, but I still would have prayed for Johnny and his ship each night. I wondered if my prayers had been answered; if the *Houston* was safe; if Johnny was safely at home. Or was he hungry too?

How wonderful it was with three chow-line meals a day! The pilot who'd parachuted out of his burning plane came into the clinic, and the way Lizzy went on about him, you would have thought he was a long-lost friend. "He looked more like an ordinary native than a second lieutenant. He said his leg was broken, but the Filipinos had taken care of it and he walked just fine. He asked for some dressings, and look what he gave me!" She displayed a couple of newly minted dimes.

His asking for the dressings was a cover-up, we discovered later. He was here on behalf of "Colonel Price," head of remarkably well-organized guerrilla forces numbering almost two hundred thousand throughout the islands. He wanted details on what the camp was like and, amiable fellow as the pilot was, none of us took notice when he talked earnestly with two men in particular before leaving.

The camp was chaos. Something had to be done quickly before it got completely out of hand, and at 10:30 that same morning, Mr. Caldwell had another announcement to make. "After so many months of internment, months filled with despondency, work, and hunger, the approaching period may prove momentous. Therefore I ask that each of you remember your obligations to yourself, to the camp, and to our country. We must each abide by the rules in existence and continue our work as an integral part of the community."

He went on to admonish the people against greed and self-interest and begged for their cooperation for the common good, pointing out that the camp as a unit could be the only means of food distribution or of reaching an outside individual in case of need.

"The blackout will continue. We will continue to have nine o'clock curfew, but there will not be a seven o'clock. You need not bow at morning roll call. In fact, you can stay in bed. Regarding the hospital, it will open for emergencies only at the usual hours."

And so the days began to settle down. At 5:30 in the afternoons, we listened to MacArthur's Voice of Freedom next to Barracks 15, and to any other stations that could be picked up. From a radio station in San Francisco, we heard a song entitled "Don't Fence Me In," and it tickled us pink even though it was "cowboy" related.

General MacArthur was making a powerful landing in Lingayen Gulf; the Japanese didn't have a chance. We knew that momentarily, triumphant American soldiers would march into Camp Freedom.

With this in mind, the administration committee moved its office into Konishi's den in Barracks

3, there to be in a better position to greet them. Little did they expect to be awakened at 2:30 A.M., 15 January, and find themselves looking back into Konishi's ugly face.

We could only guess what had prompted them to leave in such a hurry in the first place. Was it because Marinduque Island was only about sixty miles away as the crow flies, or was it because General MacArthur was following the initial Japanese tactics in landing on Luzon by way of the Lingayen Gulf? Whatever the reason may have been, the return of the Japanese was the worst blow ever. Our hopes of freedom were dashed. It had been such an exciting week, so filled with joy. The Filipinos desperately needed clothing, and as far as I was concerned, a couple of bananas, a papaya, some mongo beans, or vegetables were worth far more than clothes I had saved for happier days.

The internees who had so magically come to life during that glorious week fell back into their state of collapse, and Lieutenant Konishi took over his den. Before he retired, he released enough food for the camp's breakfast, sealed the big refrigerator, left sleepy guards at both bodegas, and promptly fell asleep.

Around four o'clock in the morning, the refrigerator stopped operating and Konishi was told that the meat would spoil if it was not repaired soon. But he simply fell asleep again.

Major Iwanata had demanded that everything

taken out of Barracks 3 and 4 be returned promptly, and then he too had gone to sleep.

"Our special orders have been completed," a weary Mr. Ito had explained. "We have returned to protect you and your people, same as before." When he asked how many of the internees had left, Mr. Caldwell assured him that everyone could be accounted for. He wanted a roll call taken but later, he said, dropping into a deep sleep on the closest bed.

The officers were more tired than the guards on duty, who caught two internees outside the fence on their way back to the camp. The next day, 16 January, another internee was caught outside, trading with a Filipino. All three internees got off with a scolding, but the Filipino was tied up outside the gate and beaten unmercifully. Next, we were told that the guards had been ordered to shoot anyone else who attempted to escape or to communicate with outsiders.

Caldwell tried to alleviate the need for internees to violate the rules by asking permission to establish a canteen where they could buy produce from the Filipinos. This was denied, and that same day, four other internees were caught outside the boundaries. They were questioned and released.

Konishi ordered that remaining parts of the carabao carcass be moved from the camp's refrigerator into the officers'. We knew that this disbursement of supplies would not be enough to keep the internees alive. The committee asked that they be allowed to continue purchasing camp food without interference, arguing that they had managed well during the week the Japanese had been away. Surprisingly, their request was granted.

During the Camp Freedom week, the administration committee had issued five kilos of uncooked rice to each internee, and now the committee again instructed Mitch to issue everyone another five kilos. But when I saw him next, Mitch was about to explode.

"Damn Konishi! He wanted to know who gave me permission to issue the rice!"

"Wasn't that turned over to the camp?"

"Of course, but the idiot said it's Japanese property and he wanted it all returned *immediately*. He says if it's not returned, I'll be charged with stealing and have to pay the supreme penalty."

"Oh, Mitch!"

"Ah, the jackass was talking through his hat."

The administration committee went to the commandant, as a result of which the Japanese took what food they thought they would need; the rest was to be turned over to the camp.

Problems continued, and Mr. Ito asked that the administration committee do everything possible to control the internees. He firmly let it be known that he would accept no further excuses: violators would be severely punished. While he was expounding on this, a Japanese sergeant came in with a message: "One of your people tried to escape and was shot."

The committee members and the two Japanese officers immediately rushed down to the ravine behind the hospital. There, about two hundred yards outside the camp boundary, was the body of an internee sprawled out on his back, a gunshot wound in his chest. "He should have listened," Mr. Caldwell said, shaking his head while Dr. Foster pronounced him dead.

His body was removed to the hospital and the burial was held that afternoon.

Another roll call was taken, and although two men were actually missing, Dr. Foster had already made out death certificates to cover for them. The following morning a visiting Japanese officer asked for another roll call. This time soldiers were sent throughout the camp, preventing anyone from going from one barracks to another in an attempt to cover for missing internees.

This same morning, previously granted purchasing privileges were revoked. "It's that dirty rat Konishi!" Mitch said. "It's the same lousy old story. Tighten the screws a little more each day. Damn it. He's the most hateful, revolting, contemptuous individual on the face of this earth!"

"It would seem so," I agreed.

"He *still* can't keep his filthy hands out of either purchasing or the camp's bodega. Not a damn thing has changed. By the time he's taken all the vegetables the garrison can eat, there's nothing left in our garden."

On Sunday, 28 January, I had just come on duty at seven o'clock in the morning when we heard a resounding rifle shot.

"Wow, that sounds as though it's over by the gate!"

"Could be," Olga said and went on with her night report, but then she stopped abruptly when she saw the doctor, stuffing his shirt into his pants, and Mr. Caldwell dash out the front door.

Major Iwanata had reason to believe someone had been sneaking out through the sawali fence that separated the husbandry corrals from the camp, and for the past few nights a watch had been stationed around its buildings. Sure enough, an internee was caught as he sneaked in under a loose part of the sawali.

Another internee was standing outside his cubicle when he heard the guard shout and fire his gun. He saw his friend Cecil fall to the pavement.

When the doctor and Caldwell arrived, they found him lying there, completely covered by a sheet, groaning and bleeding profusely, but they were stopped by guards with drawn bayonets when they tried to reach him.

"Our doctor has pronounced him dead," Iwanata said coldly.

"It's not true," Caldwell protested. "He's moving under there." But as far as the major and Mr. Ito were concerned, what difference did it make? He would be executed anyway.

"According to international law," Caldwell

276

continued, "a man should not be executed if returning to camp, but only when he is caught trying to escape."

"He disregarded my orders," Ito said with finality and walked away.

Cecil was left lying there on the road for an hour and a half before the guards dragged him over to a clump of bamboo and shot him in the back of his head, a sound heard by everyone in the hushed camp.

His body was brought over to the hospital, and when I put my hands under his shattered head to help move him into the sheet-lined coffin, parts of his brain, slimy, shiny, and squishy, fell into them.

Never had I experienced anything like this. I felt the need to wash my hands all day long, but not because of guilt. It was the horror of holding that which had stored intelligence so short a time ago. Cecil's brain, that of a young man I had seen almost daily. I had shared the boxcar ride with him from Santo Tomas. I recognized his presence by the sound of his voice and his laughter.

This time, optimism failed me. "Mitch, with all the warnings, he was being very foolish, wasn't he?"

"Yes, he was, doll." Once again, Mitch was there when I needed him.

Thereafter a second roll call was made at four o'clock. The food situation continued to worsen, mostly because of Konishi's deliberate interference, and the watery lugao had to be watered down even more just to give everyone something.

On 4 February when the "Yanks and tanks" knocked Bilibid's walls down, nearly all of the food was gone for us in Los Baños. On 5 February, while they came crashing through the front gate at Santo Tomas, it was still suicidal for a rat, a snake, or a snail to venture into our camp, much less a stray dog. For Mitzi, though, it was different. Protesting internees said, "Damn it, they shouldn't be allowed to keep the bitch. She has to be fed as well as everyone else."

"She's not taking food away from anyone except the Chapman family," others countered.

Mitzi was Mrs. Chapman's "baby." The professor and her sons repeatedly begged her to let them put the starving old animal to rest, assuring her that Mitzi would be buried and not put into the main kitchen's stews, but just the thought of it sent her into weeping and fainting spells.

Respecting her wishes, everyone had taken a hands-off policy, but least resistant to hunger's gnawing pains was Dr. Foster.

"My God, he's taken Mitzi behind the hospital with a knife in his hand!" someone shouted one day, and, although swollen by wet beriberi, the Chapman brothers came running.

Bitter words flew back and forth, but the doctor managed to slit Mitzi's throat anyway, and the brothers threatened to beat the daylights out of him when the war was over.

"What about right now?" he yelled defiantly, but when the two charged him, they were felled easily. A friend came to help, and the three of them demanded that the doctor cease and desist.

Finally, the battling men were pulled apart.

Neither the doctor nor Julius was quite as well fed as before, and we snickering nurses wondered if they would dare to dig up Mitzi's bones to make a stew of sorts.

General MacArthur's troops were heading rapidly toward Manila, we heard. They were freeing prisoners as they arrived at each POW camp. Plans were made to take them out on a Navy ship, but the dog Soochow's Marine friends refused to go without him. Dogs were not permitted aboard ship, but to solve this problem, Soochow was sent with his longtime friend the chef on a cargo plane to the Marine Corps base in San Diego.

4 February 1945 was described as follows in Bornowski's log:

Fires about Manila continue. Machine gunning and other weapons heard continuously. Low-flying U.S. planes appear over camp and visible occupants observed waving to personnel in camp. At 0930 Japanese sounded the alarm bell and everyone ordered inside buildings. At 1100, the senior Japanese noncom officer entered the warrant officer's quarters and congratulated the occupants on the success of the American forces in Manila, stating that all Japanese were leaving immediately. Gunfire heard throughout day. Japanese departed at 1245. At 1900, Yanks broke through Bilibid's north-south wall. The camp was more than elated — words cannot express the emotions of all prisoners. These soldiers had entered Manila at 1600. The officer in charge, a major, came into camp and talked with all hands. Tonight Manila is ablaze. This day will be the most unforgettable day of all of our lives.

23

RESCUE

"I'll be on night duty before long," Joyce said, "and that's when they'll be coming through the gate. I was on nights when the war started, remember?"

"It'll be when I'm on," Ellen softly insisted.

"I'm going on nights next week," Lizzy said, "and you'd better start packing. Believe me, I'm never, and I mean *never*, going to be hungry again! Not ever!"

We tried to lighten these anxious days by laughing and joking about how we walked like drunken sailors or how we had to hang onto the railing on the stairs going up or down. What better way to get a smile from our patients than to tease them, we thought.

Food had dwindled to swamp weed, and soon that was gone. "I'm beginning to think we've been forgotten," Velda said.

"Either that or our armed forces don't know we're here."

"Of course they know we are here," Miss Redecker said. "They are doing all they can."

Spindly and gaunt, she was still as neat as ever

in her faded uniform that hung loosely on her bony frame. Despite her efforts to eradicate them, gray hairs refused to be denied as each strand stood out from the rest of her neatly pinned-up hair. She too had her sick days, but according to Bobbie, that hadn't stopped her from keeping up with our service records. If that was true, mine would probably be a scorcher.

Little honest laughter was left. No one had enough gumption to carry on a difference of opinion, much less a heated dispute. Not even Mitch.

My turn came to go on nights again. There would be little to do for the dying except to offer a prayer. When death silenced their rattled breathing, their struggle was over. Lucky you, I thought. May you rest in peace.

"We might not get out of here alive," Mitch had said, and, considering what had happened last week, I didn't think dying was such a bad alternative. One night as I lay in my bed, I drowsily became aware that I wasn't breathing, and thought I could no longer hear the pulsating sound of my heart. I must be dead, I felt. What a pleasant feeling. A jazz band and an elaborate hearse . . . no wonder the Filipinos were so joyous. No more hunger, no more pain, no more war, just peace in God's heaven.

But then, darn it, I felt my heartbeat and took a breath of air. Oh, Blessed Mary, pray for me, I prayed. If God has something else in mind for me, help me to be worthy.

In the meantime, an accident that had occurred while Olga was on duty had made us all heartsick. What had seemed to be a very tepid hot-water bottle, even though protected with a worn blanket, had still been warm enough to put a blister on an undernourished baby's back. Spending so much time with this skinny little miss wasn't exactly the excitement Liz had had in mind for her week on nights, but with a lot of special attention, the infant was soon doing well enough to be seen daily as a clinic patient.

I wasn't looking forward to the long hours on nights. About the only exciting thing I could expect was one baby yet to be born, and it arrived on Sunday's day shift before I went on duty.

Now it was Friday, 23 February. Just one more night, then back on the day shift. I took the five-day-old baby into the linen closet where it was a bit warmer. "You started off on the wrong foot, didn't you, little princess?" I cooed, hurriedly changing her diaper. "You're like a defeathered chicken on Mom's sink, ready for the stew pot." As her unfocusing eyes tried to locate the sound of my voice, I added, "No need to worry. You're too tiny to make much of a meal. Maybe if we fatten you up a bit?"

Overly diluted powdered milk was a poor substitute for mother's milk, but it would have to do, and I cuddled the blanket-wrapped baby closely as I cautiously tried to bottle-feed her. The infant nipple had long passed the stage when it should have been thrown out. Not only was it too soft, the opening was much too big for such a watery formula.

"Careful there, little lady," I whispered, putting her on my shoulder to burp her.

The night passed slowly, but at last dawn was breaking. While I sat at the desk in my regulation Navy sweater, a ragged blanket over my knees, the orderlies were beginning to make preparations for early morning care.

"2/23/45," I wrote on each patient's chart, and made routine progress notes.

As the sky began to lighten, Jimmy went doggedly from bed to bed, emptying and refilling the water glasses, and another orderly came on duty. By 0650, the kitchen crew had a fire going in an effort to eke out nourishment from overworked bones. Nurses on the day's first shift were getting ready to take over.

"Will ya look at those lousy Japs?" Jimmy grumbled, as the garrison assembled in front of their quarters on Roosevelt Road.

"Yeah," I said. "We could do calisthenics, too, if we were as well fed as they are."

"Nurse, what do you suppose that is?" a patient asked.

"I can't imagine," I answered as we watched a column of pinkish smoke ascend into a windless sky. "It's colorful, to say the least."

"Sounds as though some of our planes are out there again."

"Sure does." With a yawn, I went over to check on the baby. Then suddenly —

Oh, dear God! They're going to kill us!

I grabbed the blanket-wrapped baby to protect her from the frightening sound of machine guns, and with the orderlies, I rushed over to peek out the front door at what sounded like tanks about to break down a sawali-covered fence.

I held the little princess tighter still, with the deafening roar of nine C-47s circling the camp at a low altitude. A bold banner attached to the fuselage of the lead plane read RESCUE!

Everything happened so fast. Bullets were flying in all directions. Barracks 3 and 4 were burning. Ammunition with the locked-up rifles was exploding. Then, as nine C-47s glided over the drop zone on the other side of the field, out jumped one parachutist after another, machine guns blazing.

The orderlies and I peered cautiously out the front door as the roaring sound of amtracs came closer. Down went the sawali-covered fence, in came the ungainly box-shaped vehicles with tractor treads. The first one wheeled into the hospital's circular drive; the others turned into the open area across the road. An Army major and a colonel jumped from the front of the vehicle, and after shaking hands, the colonel ran over to the other amtracs.

Magnificent, healthy American soldiers emerged from the amtrac, down the lowered ramp. Smiling and alert, our heroes had come in their camouflaged uniforms, pockets bulging with hand grenades, cartridge clips, K-rations. And those certainly weren't World War I tin hats!

"Good morning. I'm Major Briggs." Smiling at our startled faces, he quickly took in the surrounding conditions as his radioman rushed over to say he still hadn't received word from the 188th Infantry.

"They should be close by, but where are they? God, we can't stay here very long; too many hills. Too many places where the enemy can advance unseen. We've got to get these people out of here as fast as possible. Keep trying, okay?"

"Yes, sir."

"Who's in charge?" the major asked at about the same time Dr. Foster and the administration committee rushed over.

"Ma'am, what are you holding?" a soldier asked me amicably.

In all the excitement, I had forgotten about the baby. Startled, I looked at this bundle in my arms. The way I held it up and away from me, the soldier must have thought I was handing it to him, and he took her.

"Whatcha got, Gary?"

"He's got a baby! Gary's got a baby!" The poor fellow looked as embarrassed as I felt. Sheepishly I laughed along with them, and said "Thank you" when Gary put the little princess back into my arms as though she were a hot potato. Meanwhile, my pockets were filled with little Hershey bars and cigarettes, five to a pack.

Back in the ward, I delivered the baby to its mother and told the worried woman about the

American soldiers out front who'd come to take us home.

"And look what they gave us," I said, sharing the goodies.

Miss Redecker was on the scene within minutes, passing out orders right and left. Bed patients were to be loaded in the outgoing amtracs first. Since Liz had attended a burned baby daily in the clinic, she was to go with her, and Velda with my little princess.

"Miss Still, make sure the infants are dressed warmly, and take them out front, then pack your suitcase and get ready to leave."

"Yes, ma'am." In dry diapers, clean gowns, wrapped in extra blankets, and armed with warmed formulas, the two little princesses were ready.

"Here," I said to the shivering mother who had wrapped her blanket around her baby, "wear my sweater."

"We're not going to ride in these, are we?" Liz asked. "What are they?"

"Jeeps, ma'am."

"Oh, Blessed Mother of God!" And, in these strange vehicles, the four special passengers zipped ahead of the first outgoing amtracs.

Meanwhile, Major Briggs obviously was having a dilemma. He was in charge of this segment of the rescue, and giving orders to Colonel Gainor who was old enough to be his father must have been uncomfortable for them both. As they walked rapidly up Roosevelt Road, I overhead a part of their conversation.

"Sir, these people are worse off than I expected, and taking them out by land will be impossible."

"You're asking me to come back for all of them? I already have . . ." and they were out of hearing range when I rushed into Barracks 2.

"Amy, for heaven's sake, what's the matter with these people?" I said. "Don't they know we're supposed to leave in a hurry?"

Some weren't going to move until they fixed something to eat; others were frantically trying to pack their eating utensils; others insisted on taking everything they owned.

It was chilly, and before packing my suitcase I gratefully put on the sweater Clara had made for me. "Oh, heck! Where's the art pad with Dr. Jolanski's caricatures! Damn it, it's in my trunk! I'll be right back!"

"Dottie, the bodega is on fire."

Sick at heart, Amy and I hurried out as fast as we could, but by now the amtracs were gone. Along with Bobbie, we sat dejectedly on the hospital's front steps.

A soldier yelled, "Major Briggs says if these folks refuse to move, we're to start burning the barracks!"

Everything was going wrong. Watching what had been home go up in flames was bad enough. I was dreadfully tired. Gone was my irreplaceable art book, and forgive me merciful God, I thought, but right now I don't give a damn if I live or die!

Mitch and Hank joined us, both lamenting the

loss of the kitchen's cart to the flames. "Now we'll all have to carry our belongings."

"Everyone over here!" the major shouted. Then he asked a soldier, "Is everyone out?" He asked the radioman if he had had any luck yet. No, he hadn't. A Filipino lad offered to carry the radioman's generator.

We would find out later that this lad had been partially responsible for our liberation. He had appeared out of nowhere and had asked the major when they were going to Los Baños. "You, young man, are coming with us," had been the answer.

We would also learn that two men who had escaped from Los Baños during Camp Freedom week had played an important role in the rescue. They had helped prepare a map of the camp and had told of the camp's routine and the condition of the people.

An elaborate plan had been devised involving the help of the guerrillas, but almost none of the officers in charge knew what their own or anyone else's role actually would be until a few hours before the rescue. Then, just minutes before it started, this dispatch had apparently come in:

- URGENT -
RECEIVED RELIABLE INFORMATION
THAT LOS BAÑOS IS SCHEDULED FOR
MASSACRE ON 23 FEB
W. C. Price
COLONEL GSC (GUERR)
CHIEF OF STAFF

"Your attention, please!" Briggs shouted. "It's going to be a long walk down to the lake! We'll take it as easy as we can, but we can't loiter! You are to stay close together! We'll be around you on all sides! There may be snipers out there, and if firing begins, you are to lie face-down on the ground! Is that understood?"

"Sir, we checked the barracks, and they've all been torched!"

"Good! Let's go!"

The major and Carson led the way, and with the C-47s circling overhead, the major waved his thanks to the lead plane.

"Any trouble with your Ghost platoon, Lieutenant?"

"Only that moments before the exact time, a Jap guard at a pillbox must have heard our soldier come up behind him, but his wild shooting got him nowhere but dead."

"Can you believe this?" the major asked, showing the dispatch to Carson.

"Good Lord! Looks as though we didn't get here too soon."

"I wonder if MacArthur knows that the Japs starve prisoners who are about to be executed, and that's what we have on our hands."

While this conversation was going on, Bobbie, Hank, Mitch, and I stumbled along with the others. A segment of the major's soldiers and Filipino guerrillas were cordoned around us. Those who mingled among us gave assistance as needed. Their words of encouragement made us feel safe, yet they obviously weren't as confident as we were. We heard sporadic shots — from our rifles or theirs? The soldiers remained calm, but we knew that no sound escaped their notice, no movement of the grass, bushes, or trees went unseen.

The amtracs' trail left the paved road, and the dirt slowed us down more than ever. After a while the major motioned us aside to let two repaired amtracs pass. The first one was filled with priests; the second with nuns. Impatient Virgin was painted on the side of the nuns' amtrac, which was worth a tired chuckle.

After a while, Mitch said, "This morning I had a surprise for you and Amy. I brought in several ears of corn."

"Did you really?" But just thinking about food brought about the sickening sweetness of the little Hershey bar that kept regurgitating now and then.

"Last night one of the guards took several of us over to a different warehouse where rice had been stored. We filled sacks with whatever palay we could find, and on the way back he let us see what we could find in an already harvested corn-field."

Farther along the trail, Amy jumped at the sight of a dead Japanese soldier off to the side, and the major and the lieutenant urged us to move along faster. If one Jap had managed to get this far away from the camp, they said, there could be others.

"Too bad it's not Konishi," Mitch said. "Wish

I hadn't seen this guy like that. Last night he knew I was having a bad time carrying that miserable sack of rice, so he handed me his rifle and carried it himself."

On we trod until finally, we sighed with relief when we reached the narrow beach on Mayondon Point. I sat down on a log, kicked off my shoes, and rubbed my tired feet. Solicitous soldiers wandered among us, and Bobbie asked one paratrooper, "What's going on in the States?"

"Pretty busy back there."

Soon several people were questioning him. "Who won the presidential election last November?"

"Who else? Roosevelt."

"What outfit are you with?"

"The 11th Airborne Division," he said, and, after confusing us with the different branches of the division, he talked about jumps they had made on Leyte and on the Tagatay Ridge as though it were no more dangerous than diving off a swimming pool's high platform. But even as he spoke, his eyes remained constantly on the alert.

"Amy," I said finally, "I'm going to lie down over there under the coconut tree." And, with the monotonous sound of the C-47s circling overhead, I drifted off to sleep.

We had been on the beach for almost two hours, and soldiers had been spaced in an arc around the beach all this time. Now sporadic gunfire could be heard, and artillery shells that lobbed overhead and dropped harmlessly into the lake farther out were getting closer.

Finally the first amtrac came onto the beach, and a photographer from Time Life was right behind Colonel Gainor when he jumped ashore. The major was beside himself as he greeted the colonel. "Well, look who's here!"

Several people, including Mitch, clustered around the photographer as he busily snapped pictures while he talked with them.

"Who's that?" Amy asked.

"I think he was one of the orderlies in Santo Tomas," Bobbie said, going over to find out while Amy and I walked over to the first amtrac that came up on the beach.

"Is it okay for us to come aboard?" I asked the two soldiers sitting up front.

"Any time," said one.

"What are those pins on your collars? Not military, are they?" said the other.

"Navy Nurse Corps," I answered, taking off my sweater. "It gets a little warm down here, doesn't it?"

"Wanna come up here?"

"Oh, could we?"

"Sure, come on."

Soldiers anxiously herded internees into the amtracs as each one came ashore, the artillery shells getting closer all the time. The last amtrac was hardly a safe distance away when Japanese soldiers swarmed onto the narrow beach, but, miracle of miracles, not a single soldier or civilian was left behind.

The cool breeze was refreshing, and it was reassuring to see the C-47s circling overhead in the bright blue sky as Amy and I sat on top of the amtrac in the shade of her ragged old umbrella.

"Nurse, one of the fellows down there passed out."

"Oh my goodness, is there any way you can bring him up here?"

"Sure thing." They put the unconscious internee between Amy and me, his head resting on my arm. One of the soldiers held the umbrella over us while Amy put my sweater over him and monitored his pulse. The photographer jumped up to take a few shots.

"Is he all right?" one of the soldiers asked anxiously.

"He'll be fine. He's been hospitalized many times. It was too hot for him down there and he fainted." As the stricken man regained consciousness, we put him into a more comfortable upright position in my arms for the rest of the slow and noisy trip.

24

GETTING HOME

After a dramatic rescue such as this, sequential events were more or less anticlimatic. Charlie and Earl were anxiously waiting for Mitch on the beach, because Charlie had hitched a ride to Nichols Army airfield and finagled passage on a cargo plane. The last time I saw Mitch was on Mayondon Point. We didn't have a chance to say good-bye, and although it was like losing my right arm, it was just as well.

I was thoroughly exhausted when I arrived at the New Bilibid Prison at Muntinlupa, and while Miss Redecker and Julia were talking to a couple of men up front, I stretched out on one of the benches and fell asleep.

A few hours later Julia came over to awaken me, saying that the Red Cross had mail from home for the internees. I went over to where they had several tables set up with mail in alphabetical order. There was one from my mother, and it was not as restricted as had been previous letters. There were also tables with standard Red Cross letter-writing forms, pencils, envelopes, and workers who could help us to write.

This was the first of many adjustments I would have to make in a world that had changed so rapidly. Working with an Army doctor and corpsman was quite a revelation. So many new drugs and sterile administration sets designed for treating casualties on the spot. So many disposables, and it hurt to see presterile intravenous tubing and single-use needles thrown into the trash.

And food! It was served cafeteria-style in the prison's mess hall, so much, ever so much. To see the large empty cans of Spam being tossed away was unbelievable! How could the soldiers complain about Spam, of all things? But listening to them, I realized they were sick of the same thing day after day.

"What'll you have, miss?" the man behind the counter said. Still sick to my stomach from the chocolate candy and cigarettes the paratroopers had given me, I asked if that was milk they were serving. Yes it was, made from powdered milk, and I asked for that and a slice of bread. I needed something to wash down the vitamins of all kinds that were being distributed in wholesale lots. I knew I could always come back for more, since the the line was open around the clock.

In the meantime, General MacArthur had sent his regards to our little Navy group, along with a few copies of the amateurish newspaper the *Manila Free Philippines*. In the one dated 27 February 1945, the following appeared on the editorial page:

THE LOS BAÑOS COUP

For careful planning, daring execution and brilliant results, this war offers few parallels to the rescue of 2,200 American, British and other Allied internees from Los Baños concentration camp last week. This achievement marks a new high in MacArthur's campaign to liberate the Philippines. As American paratroopers dropped from the skies to annihilate the Jap Garrison in the camp, huge amphibious tractors came roaring out of Laguna de Bay and smashed their way into the camp grounds. The internees and the paratroopers were loaded into the tractors which rolled back through enemy machine gun fire to the edge of Laguna de Bay, plunged into the water and carried their cargo safely behind American lines. Most astonishing of all, the operation was carried out with total military casualties of two dead and two wounded, while two internees were slightly wounded. "Nothing could be more satisfying to a soldier's heart than this rescue," General MacArthur said. "I am deeply grateful. God was with us today. The American and Filipino people are also deeply grateful for the organized genius and efficient execution which have so successfully defeated the Japanese at every step on the long road back, a road which will end in Tokyo."

We stayed here with our patients until Army nurses from Samar could relieve us, and then another ten days until they and our patients were comfortable with one another. It wasn't easy to say good-bye to my internee friends, especially Hank, Allen, Heidi, Rick, and Andy and his delightful wife, Diane. Nor was it easy to say good-bye to the orderlies and nurses' aides who had been such a part of my life for the past two years. Nonetheless, on we went to the University of Santo Tomas, taking Clara, Felicia, and Helena with us.

Here it was more rich food and scads of vitamin pills. Army nurses from Samar had already relieved Captain Crawford and her ex-POW nurses, who were already back in the States. We learned about the horror experienced by internees who had been in the crossfire for days before one of the three American monoplanes flew at a low altitude, wings dipping. How exciting it must have been when one of the pilots dropped his goggles carrying a bold message — "Roll out the barrel." The only way to get the Japanese out of the compound had been to grant them permission to go out the gate unmolested.

On 5 February, American troops had moved into Bilibid. *Liberated!* Japanese snipers had still been about, bullets flying, fires getting closer. At 2100 hours stretcher cases had been put on Army jeeps, and all personnel able to walk had begun filing out of Bilibid, to be picked up a half mile farther along and taken to Ang Tibay Shoe Factory in Balintawak, general headquarters for the U.S. Army forces.

We nurses were delayed another ten days before Admiral Kinkaid's personal plane landed on a bomb-pitted runway on Manila's Nielson airfield, there to take all of us, including Clara, Felicia, and Helena, to the admiral's headquarters in Leyte.

As we flew over Manila Bay, we could see the horrendous damage the Japanese navy had inflicted as they attempted to hold the city at all costs. I didn't know it at the time, but Pete Dalton, on one of the cruisers, knew I was a freed prisoner of war and had hoped to see me before we left.

We could see our beautiful ships among the sunken Japanese ships; the Cañacao Navy Hospital, which seemed to be intact; and Lake Taal. We marveled at how big the Laguna de Bay was, and before we knew it, the plane was landing on Leyte.

Now it was one blinding flashbulb after another as we neatly posed with Admiral Kinkaid in front of his tent, until I messed up the arrangement for further pictures by fainting. Sitting on a chair off to one side, I listened to the admiral telling the others his Seventh Fleet was "MacArthur's Navy."

The paymaster went out of his mind trying to figure out how much back pay each of the Big Three might have, based on their probable rank and longevity. We were no longer to be addressed as Miss but as Ensign, with honest-to-goodness gold-backed American money in our pockets.

"Ensign Still? A lieutenant would like to see you in the reaction tent."

Johnny? It couldn't be. It turned out to be an ensign I had dated once, and what a bore. The only redeeming thing about his visit was a chair to sit on away from all the commotion, while I listened to him brag about having married a beautiful Filipino woman, as though I had had my chance and lost it. Thank goodness, Julia rescued me by coming to say that lunch was about to be served in the Quonset hut mess hall.

Here, several long sheet-covered utility tables had been arranged for a special luncheon. Miss Redecker sat at the head table next to Admiral Kinkaid, and other officers mixed in among the rest of us. We and our hosts were in different worlds mentally, but when Liz laughingly said something about attending a top-level event like this dressed in made-over dungaree uniforms, that lessened the tension considerably.

"What's the matter, Dottie?" Joyce said. "Aren't you going to finish your steak?"

"It tastes so good, but it's much too rich. I just can't eat it." A few bites of mashed potatoes, peas, and a light dessert were all I could handle.

"Pass it over," she said.

Our hosts were clearly trying to entertain us, going out of their way to keep the conversation light and cheerful. But I had to know about the

Houston. Toward the end of our delightful luncheon, I told the two officers next to me that I'd had a special friend on the ship and asked if they could tell me what had happened to it and the Asiatic fleet.

It had all happened so long ago, it was probably an unfair question, but as they said good-bye, they advised me to be philosophical about my friend's welfare. He could have been one of the survivors when the *Houston* had gone down at the Battle of the Java Sea, in February 1942.

Our visit over, the admiral apologized for having to send us on an unlined C-47 cargo plane, and off we went. At the Army hospital on Samar, we dressed in winter uniforms borrowed from the Army nurses. After that our C-47 headed for Pearl Harbor, island-hopping along the way with stops on Guam and Kwajalein.

At the naval air base in Pearl Harbor, photographers asked us to come out of the plane a second time. By then the chief nurse at Aeia Naval Hospital and her assistant had arrived to greet us with leis, and, surprisingly, captains Roth and Porter were there too. But what should have been a festive occasion was dulled as we travel-weary nurses stood self-consciously in the terminal. After the first few words, there wasn't much left to say.

I had had dinner in Manila a couple of times with fatherly Captain Porter, a commander then, after the dependents had left and the Asiatic fleet was out on maneuvers. I was glad to see him again. He asked how well the doctors out there held up, and I told him how much I admired doctors Stewart, Baker, Kleinfeldt, and some of the others. I also said how disappointed I had been in some of them.

"Oh, my goodness," I added, "who am I to be disappointed in any one of them? Being a prisoner of war brings out the best and the worst in all of us, and if there is anyone I should be disappointed in, it's me."

"You mustn't be so hard on yourself, young lady. I guess I won't know how I would react until I have been tried, will I?"

At last, we were driven to the Nurses' Quarters at Aeia Naval Hospital. There we experienced our first hot baths in nearly four years. We slept on coil-spring mattresses and had hand lotions, clean-smelling colognes, bath powder, and current magazines at our disposal.

It was dinnertime before our borrowed Army attire had been replaced with borrowed Navy Nurse Corps uniforms. All clean and hair combed, we were nevertheless a gloomy-looking lot as we sat uneasily at the dining room tables.

Over the next few days we rested, shopped, and groomed ourselves. Miss Redecker's hair went back to its previous jet-black color, and the rest of us got hair cuts and permanents as desired. Proud of the Lt. (jg.) stripes on our dress uniform jackets, we were ready to face more photographers' flashbulbs and reporters' interviews.

After a radio brocast to the folks back home, it was off to Oakland, California, in comfortable passenger seats. We had to disembark twice, again, at the request of photographers, then still more flashbulbs and interviews in the terminal.

"Lieutenant Still? An officer in the lounge would like to talk to you." Johnny? Could it really be Johnny this time? In the maze of uniformed men and women, I couldn't see either him or anyone else I knew until someone said, "Hi ya, Dixie." My brother-in-law!

"My goodness, Dave, aren't you handsome in your Army Air Force uniform! No wonder Mom said Paula didn't see much of you these days!"

He had been stationed in Iceland and was being transferred to somewhere on the East Coast. He was now on R and R and on his way to Long Beach, where Paula and my nephew were staying temporarily.

The following days were exciting yet trying as, like the others, I became a full lieutenant. We all got physical examinations at the Oakknoll Naval Hospital, and Liz was immediately transferred to a special hospital in New York.

Jeanette MacDonald sang for us at a cocktail party; at a dinner party Mrs. Nimitz told us the admiral was sorry he had missed us but sent his regards; San Francisco opened its arms to us. After a final luncheon at the St. Francis Drake Hotel in Knob Hill, it was a ninety-day recuperative leave for all of us.

———

Many years later, I would learn that despite the hardships we had endured, all of the Army nurses and the eleven Navy nurses came home.

25

ADJUSTING

It was good to be home, but both my mother and father had aged considerably since I had seen them last. Paula and my nephew had been home while Dave was overseas, and undoubtedly she had been a godsend to our parents. Obviously it hadn't been easy for them. Undoubtedly Mother and Dad had dreaded official communications asking for photos and other information about me. How awful it must have been to receive that telegram informing them I was missing in action. Letters from the internees who had been repatriated from Los Baños had been a big help, but there had always been the possibility of getting one that said, "Your government is sorry to inform you that your daughter (or husband) is . . ." Then the silver star on display in the window (meaning a member of the family was in the service) would have been replaced by a gold one.

I hadn't been home long before my presence was known, and the publicity bewildered them. They found it difficult to understand me. I guess it was because I was restless and missed the camaraderie of the nurses and close friends in Los

Baños. I tried not to think about Mitch, but I missed him. I went to masses to pray for Johnny and others out there who had not been as fortunate as I. Being a guest speaker was something to do.

I had come home to a different world. From the quiet town I had known, Long Beach had changed into a beehive of activity, with service men and women everywhere.

In the officers' lounge at the Navy base, I had cocktails with some of the prewar Cañacao nurses I had known out there. I saw Dr. Kleinfeldt again and met his family at a luncheon. We had much to talk about.

"Lieutenant Still, will you be our guest speaker at the Rotary Club luncheon?"

"The chamber of commerce needs a speaker . . ."

"CBS is putting on a radio show in Hollywood, and you are invited to . . ."

"Will you speak to the workers at the shipyard?"

One day the public-relations officer said he was going to cover the arrival of the ship that was bringing freed civilians from the Philippines, and would I like to go along.

It was good to see my old friends, all wearing the wrinkled clothes they had saved so long to come home in.

"Oh, Dottie, dear!" Heidi said as we hugged, Rick at her elbow. "We're so glad to be home!"

Everyone else was too, of course, and the PR officer busily clicked away. It was wonderful to see them all.

But there were other kinds of visits too. "My dear Lieutenant! I love your display of ribbons! I'm dying to hear what it was like! Do tell me! And darling, don't spare the gory details!"

"It was rough at times, but . . ."

"Oh yes, I know exactly what you mean. You wouldn't believe what we've been through. It has been rough here, let me tell you. We've had to stand in line for hours to get meat stamps and gasoline stamps. Did you get your food stamps, dear? And have you tried to find nylons? They're simply not available." And so on.

One welcome invitation was to go out to dinner with Pete Dalton. As he requested, I dressed in my uniform with the assortment of honorary ribbons. I couldn't believe it when he showed up as a Navy enlisted man!

"Pete, I can't go out with you in an officer's uniform!"

"My dear girl, this is a wartime Navy, and no one gives a damn."

"I do," I said, and changed into a dress.

Pete was getting out of the service on a disability. He was good company, and I continued to see him off and on. Seeing how miserable I was, he asked me to marry him. A nice guy, yes, but that was out of the question.

Then came the New York trip. "Lieutenant

Still, you are to represent the Navy Nurse Corps at the *New York Tribune*'s Annual Forum," I was told.

I felt at a loss in the sumptuous Waldorf Astoria Hotel, where, in a crowded auditorium, each of us four military women was introduced and our accomplishments read. There was also a corpsman, a representative of the five men who had planted the American flag on Iwo Jima's Mount Suribachi on 23 February, the same day I had been rescued.

Until now I had been proud to represent the Navy Nurse Corps, but this time I felt insignificant and unworthy. These people represented the real heroes and heroines, not me. I had simply sat the war out, being neither particularly brave nor courageous. People wouldn't praise me like this if they knew the truth.

"We may not come out of this alive," Mitch had said. But I hadn't died, and at this point, I didn't like myself at all.

I called California. "Pete? This is Dottie. Do you still want to get married?"

Two days later: "Pete, I just can't do it. I'm so mixed up."

I can't say that I was always so depressed. We went on to Washington, D.C., where there were so many interesting things to see. I shared a publicity event with Paul Phillips, and, gaunt and sickly though he was, he still had that infectious smile. "Sorry I couldn't bring your jacket back,"

I joked, which got a laugh.

Then came 6 August. It must have been a worrisome decision for President Truman when he gave the green light for the first atomic bomb to be used on Hiroshima. When a second bomb was released over Nagasaki on 9 August, Japan capitulated.

The official Japanese surrender was on 2 September 1945, and our nation's newspaper coverage was tremendous. General MacArthur was in his glory as he accepted Japan's surrender aboard the battleship *Missouri*. Sailors in their dress whites looked down to the main deck, where high-ranking Army and Navy officers stood by. General MacArthur affixed his signature after those of Japan's military warlords, and General Wainwright stood in an honorary position behind him.

At last the war was over! V-J Day celebrations were the wildest ever throughout the country, well documented by the Time Life magazines. My prayers for the war to end had been answered. The Navy Nurse Corps celebrated in Bethesda, where I was able to ask the superintendent if our former chief nurse had submitted our service records. Yes she had, she said, but with a twinkle in her eye, she added that somehow they had been lost.

And then more good news came: in a Red Cross magazine, I saw a picture of Johnny and some of his shipmates who had been prisoners in Japan. The story was all about *Houston* survivors.

Could Johnny still be alive? He had given me his mother's address in Reno years ago, so I wrote to ask if she had heard anything about him. She had, and now I knew that indeed all my prayers had been answered. I sent a welcome-home note for him through her.

Shortly after this, I ran into one of his shipmates. From what he said, Johnny had been talking about our relationship as though I were quite a conquest. I couldn't believe it!

But then Johnny came to see me in Bethesda. He looked more handsome than ever, and was just as charming. In his usual style, he had a gift for me, a beautiful bronze-colored watch whose chain-link band fit my wrist perfectly. I told him what his shipmate had said, and he started to laugh! I dashed up to my room, about to break down into tears. I never saw Johnny again.

Christmas Day brought something I will always treasure. Written on blue stationery topped by the Navy Nurse Corps emblem, the following was slipped under my door:

December 25, 1945
Dear Dottie,

A year ago this Christmas,
We were dreaming of the day
When we could really celebrate
In good old USA.

Remember the night the Padres sang

Songs camouflaged to tell
The news we wanted so to hear,
How they made us feel, "All's well"?

Remember the babe in the manger
Modeled of sand and clay?
'Twas a work of art and as beautiful
As any we'll see today.

Remember the toys made for the children,
And the carolers who sang carols of old?
How we forgot about gifts that are purchased,
But greetings were meant from the soul?

Now we're home and have the materials
To have a grand and glorious day,
I hope we'll always remember
The spirit shared a year ago today.

Sincerely,
Amy

The nation's capital was losing its luster for me, and a Christmas card from Mitch didn't help. I wasn't really important to anyone in particular, I felt, least of all to myself.

"Pete, do you still want to get married?"

Returning to civilian life was another difficult adjustment. Pete and I bought a cute house in North Hollywood, and I picked up how-to books ranging from cooking to housekeeping to gardening. Before the year was out, it was yet another adjustment when our first baby was born. She really wasn't as fragile as a china doll.

After three years, like many other returning GIs, we moved away from North Hollywood out to the countryside. Pete built an egg ranch, and along came another baby. By now I was more comfortable as a mother and housewife, but I was still miserable.

Through all of this I could hide from public relations more or less, but not from myself. I resented Pete for being so damned patient with me. Why didn't he just tell me to straighten up and fly right?

Then everything changed one Sunday afternoon, when Mitch and his family dropped by unexpectedly. Outwardly it was a pleasant visit, but when Pete quietly suggested I invite them to stay for dinner, I told him I just didn't feel up to it.

They couldn't leave too soon, as far as I was concerned. I kept my emotions tightly hidden while they were there. Later, while Pete was watching the football game on our black-and-white TV, I hurried out to busy myself in the egg room. As I was sorting and packing eggs, Father John's "I wouldn't like to see you get hurt" kept flashing through my mind. But my heart had been broken, and I cried like I would never be able to stop while I kept cracking the eggs. This shouldn't have happened, I kept thinking, and then I would burst into renewed tears.

Pete came looking for me when the football game was over.

"What's the matter, honey?"

"Oh, nothing," I said, not looking at him. But he knew better, and he quietly held me in his arms. Finally I couldn't help but tell him why I was so upset. Wiping away my tears, he patiently said, "Let's bury the past once and for all. Okay?"

That wasn't easy. I deliberately stopped exchanging Christmas cards with Mitch, which helped. With the passage of time, I learned to accept myself, to laugh and joke, and to really be a wife and mother. Pete sold the ranch and went back to his former job as a sound technician with a CBS television team.

Then came another adjustment, a dreadfully traumatic one. In our ten years together, I learned to appreciate what a fine man I had married. But then, while he and the cameraman were in San Francisco covering the Republican convention that nominated Dwight D. Eisenhower for president, Pete died suddenly of a coronary hemorrhage, leaving me with an unborn infant.

By this time my parents were dead, and I seldom saw Paula and Dave. Fortunately I inherited Pete's wonderful family. His closest cousin encouraged me to buy a house near theirs, a block away from a sandy beach in San Diego County. Here I built a new life for our little family.

It was not all peaches and cream: there were times when I was mad at Pete for leaving me like this. Mitch, where are you when I need you?

Johnny? It hurt to even think about him.

Sick of children's monosyllables, I got a job in a doctor's office. As my youngest child grew older, I went to work in a local hospital as the central service supervisor. The children grew to adulthood, and then came the empty-nest syndrome, an adjustment with a different twist.

"Hello?" I said, answering the telephone one day, expecting to hear from one of my children. I could hardly believe what I heard.

"Dottie? Is that you, doll?"

"Mitch?" Stunned, I sat down on a chair.

And what nicer words to hear than those he could finally say: "I don't care what your old man says, doll, I love you."

ABOUT THE AUTHOR

After recovering from the beriberi she contracted while a POW, Dorothy Still Danner traveled in support of U.S. Navy public relations activities. She left the Navy in 1947, was married, and raised three children. A grandmother of six, she now resides in Boise, Idaho.